C++ Programming

C++ Programming

Emily Jones

CLANRYE
INTERNATIONAL
www.clanryeinternational.com

Clanrye International,
750 Third Avenue, 9ᵗʰ Floor,
New York, NY 10017, USA

ISBN: 978-1-64726-102-3

Cataloging-in-Publication Data

C++ programming / Emily Jones.
p. cm.
Includes bibliographical references and index.
ISBN: 978-1-64726-102-3
1. C++ (Computer program language). 2. Object-oriented programming languages.
I. Jones, Emily.
QA76.73.C153 C25 2022
005.133--dc23

For information on all Clanrye International publications
visit our website at www.clanryeinternational.com

Table of Contents

Preface

This book is a culmination of my many years of practice in this field. I attribute the success of this book to my support group. I would like to thank my parents who have showered me with unconditional love and support and my peers and professors for their constant guidance.

C++ is a general purpose programming language that is used for computer programming. It has various object-oriented, generic and functional features in addition to facilities for low-level memory manipulation. C++ is always implemented as a compiled language. The two main components of C++ language are direct mapping of hardware features that is primarily provided by the C subset, and zero-overhead abstractions that are based on those mappings. The C++ standard consists of two parts that are the core language and the standard library. It is well suited for resource-constrained software and large systems. This book traces the progress of C++ Programming and highlights some of its key concepts and applications. While understanding the long-term perspectives of the topics, it makes an effort in highlighting their impact as a modern tool for the growth of the discipline. This book will provide comprehensive knowledge to the readers.

The details of chapters are provided below for a progressive learning:

Chapter – Introduction

C++ is an object-oriented general purpose high-level programming language which is used to build complex programs. There are a number of components in C++ like data types, variable types, loop types, functions, decision making statements, arrays, strings, pointer, etc. This is an introductory chapter which will briefly introduce all the significant components of C++.

Chapter – General Concepts of C++

C++ is a vast field of language comprising concepts of classes, auto-linking, Argument-Dependent Name Lookup, header file, one definition rule, run-time type information, sequence point, single compilation unit, undefined behavior, virtual function cells, etc. This chapter has been carefully written to provide an easy understanding of the varied concepts of C++.

Chapter – C++ Language Extension

An extension is a programming language interpreter provided by an application program, used by the user to write macros or even a whole program. Cilk Plus, AspectC++, C++/CLI, C++/CX, CUDA C/C++, etc. are some of the C++ extensions that fall under this domain. This chapter discusses in detail these C++ language extensions.

Chapter – C++ Compilers

Software which is used to convert high-level programming language code into a low-level machine readable code is termed as a compiler. AMD optimizing C/C++ compiler, Clang, HP aC++, Intel C++ Compiler, Visual C++, etc. are some examples of the C++ compiler. The topics elaborated in this chapter will help in gaining a better perspective about the compilers in C++.

Chapter – Algorithms in C++

An algorithm is a piece of code which takes input from the user and produces a desirable output. It uses a set of rules and protocols for performing calculations and solving a problem. Heap sort, merge sort, quick sort, radix sort, bubble sort, etc. are some of the algorithms used in C++. This chapter closely examines these C++ algorithms to provide an extensive understanding of the subject.

Chapter – Data Structures in C++

A data structure is defined as a collection of data which can be easily accessed, managed, combined and modified. C++ uses data structures like stack data structure, queue data structure, heaps, hash tables, two-three trees, binary trees, stacks, linked lists, etc. All these diverse C++ data structures have been carefully analyzed in this chapter.

Chapter – C++ Dialects

A programming language dialect is a small extension of the language that does not changes its nature, but makes it compatible with other programming platforms. This chapter delves into dialects such as Charm++, Embedded C++, R++, Sieve C++ Parallel Programming System, μC++, etc. to provide in-depth understanding of C++ dialects.

Emily Jones

1

Introduction

C++ is an object-oriented general purpose high-level programming language which is used to build complex programs. There are a number of components in C++ like data types, variable types, loop types, functions, decision making statements, arrays, strings, pointer, etc. This is an introductory chapter which will briefly introduce all the significant components of C++.

C++

C++ is a programming language developed by Bjarne Stroustrup in 1979 at Bell Labs. C++ is regarded as a middle-level language, as it comprises a combination of both high-level and low-level language features. It is a superset of C, and that virtually any legal C program is a legal C++ program. C++ runs on a variety of platforms, such as Windows, Mac OS, and the various versions of UNIX.

It is a language that is:

- Statically typed: A programming language is claimed to use static typing when type checking is performed during compile-time as opposed to run-time.

- Compiled: A compiled language is a programming language whose implementations are typically compilers (translators that generate machine code from source code), and not interpreters (step-by-step executors of source code, where no pre-runtime translation takes place).

- General-purpose: A general-purpose language could be a language that is generally applicable across application domains, and lacks specialized options for a specific domain. This is in contrast to a domain-specific language (DSL), which is specialized to a particular application domain.

- Case-sensitive: C++ is case sensitive, ie, all identifiers, keywords, etc mean different things when they are in the different case.

- Free-form: A free-form language is a programming language in which the positioning of characters on the page in program text is insignificant.

- Procedural Programming: A procedural programming language is an important programming language whose programs have the ability to be primarily structured in terms of reusable procedures, e.g. subroutines and/or functions.

- Object-oriented Programming: Object-oriented programming (OOP) is a programming paradigm based on the concept of "objects", which may contain data, in the form of fields, often known as attributes; and code, in the form of procedures, often known as methods.

- Generic Programming: Generic programming is a style of computer programming in which algorithms are written in terms of types to-be-specified-later that are then instantiated when needed for specific types provided as parameters.

C++ Basic Syntax

Tokens

Tokens are the smallest meaningful symbols in the language. In other words, tokens are the minimal chunk of program that has meaning to the compiler. The following table lists all tokens used in C++ programming.

Token Type	Description/Purpose	Example
keywords	Words with special meaning to the compiler	`int, double, for, auto`
Identifiers	Names of things that are not built into the language	`cout, std, x, myFunction`
Literals	Basic constant values whose value is specified directly in the source code	`"Hello, world!", 24.3, 0, 'c'`
Operators	Mathematical or logical operations	`+, -, &&, %, <<`
Punctuation/Separators	Punctuation defining the structure of a program	`{ } ( ), ;`
Whitespace	Spaces of various sorts; ignored by the compiler	`Spaces, tabs, newlines, comments`

Escape Sequences

An escape sequence is a symbol used to represent a special character in a text literal. Here are all the C++ escape sequences which you can include in strings that you want to manipulate:

Escape Sequence	Represented Character
\a	System bell (beep sound)
\b	Backspace
\f	Formfeed (page break)
\n	Newline (line break)
\r	"Carriage return" (returns cursor to start of line)
\\	Backslash

\t	Tab
\'	Single quote character
\"	Double quote character
\some integer x	The character represented by x

Comments

Comments help the person writing a program, and anyone else who must read the source file, understand what's going on. The compiler ignores comments, so they do not add to the file size or execution time of the executable program.

Syntax

- Single line comments start with a double slash symbol (//) and terminate at the end of the line. A comment can start at the beginning of the line or on the same line following a program statement.

  ```
  // this is single line comment
  ```

- Multiline comments begins with the /* character pair and ends with */ (not with the end of the line).

- ```
  /* this
  ```

- ```
  is a
  ```

- ```
  very
  ```

- ```
  very long
  ```

- ```
  multiline
  ```

- ```
  comment
  ```

- ```
  */
  ```

- ```
  /* this can also be used in single line comment */
  ```

Directives

Directives are not part of the basic C++ language, but they're necessary anyway. For example, in "Helloworld" program the two lines after comment are directives. The first is a preprocessor directive, and the second is a using directive.

A preprocessor directive is an instruction to the compiler. For example, in preprocessor directive

```
#include <iostream>
```

#include tells the preprocessor to include the contents of another file, here the iostream file, which defines the procedures for input/output.

Before going with using directive, let's look at namespace stuff. A namespace is a part of the program in which certain names are recognized; outside of the namespace they're unknown. A C++ program can be divided into different namespaces.

If we want to access an identifier defined in a namespace, we tell the compiler to look for it in that namespace using the scope resolution operator (::) as

```
std::cout << "Hello, world!\n";
```

or, we can use using directive as

```
using namespace std;
```

which says that all the program statements that follow are within the std namespace.

C++ Data Types

All variables use data-type during declaration to restrict the type of data to be stored. Therefore, we can say that data types are used to tell the variables the type of data it can store. Whenever a variable is defined in C++, the compiler allocates some memory for that variable based on the data-type with which it is declared. Every data type requires a different amount of memory.

Data types in C++ are mainly divided into three types:

- Primitive Data Types: These data types are built-in or predefined data types and can be used directly by the user to declare variables. Example: int, char, float, bool etc. Primitive data types available in C++ are:
  - Integer,
  - Character,
  - Boolean,
  - Floating Point,
  - Double Floating Point,
  - Valueless or Void,
  - Wide Character.
- Derived Data Types: The data-types that are derived from the primitive or built-in data-types are referred to as Derived Data Types. These can be of four types namely:
  - Function,
  - Array,
  - Pointer,
  - Reference.

- Abstract or User-Defined Data Types: These data types are defined by user itself. Like, defining a class in C++ or a structure. C++ provides the following user-defined datatypes:

  ○ Class,

  ○ Structure,

  ○ Union,

  ○ Enumeration,

  ○ Typedef defined DataType.

Here, we discuss the primitive data types available in C++:

- Integer: Keyword used for integer data types is int. Integers typically requires 4 bytes of memory space and ranges from -2147483648 to 2147483647.

- Character: Character data type is used for storing characters. Keyword used for character data type is char. Characters typically requires 1 byte of memory space and ranges from -128 to 127 or 0 to 255.

- Boolean: Boolean data type is used for storing boolean or logical values. A boolean variable can store either *true* or *false*. Keyword used for boolean data type is bool.

- Floating Point: Floating Point data type is used for storing single precision floating point values or decimal values. Keyword used for floating point data type is float. Float variables typically requires 4 byte of memory space.

- Double Floating Point: Double Floating Point data type is used for storing double precision floating point values or decimal values. Keyword used for double floating point data type is double. Double variables typically require 8 byte of memory space.

- Void: Void means without any value. Void datatype represents a valueless entity. Void data type is used for those functions which do not return a value.

- Wide Character: Wide character data type is also a character data type but this data type has size greater than the normal 8-bit datatype. Represented by wchar_t. It is generally 2 or 4 bytes long.

Datatype Modifiers

As the name implies, datatype modifiers are used with the built-in data types to modify the length of data that a particular data type can hold. Data type modifiers available in C++ are:

- Signed,

- Unsigned,

- Short,

- Long.

Below table summarizes the modified size and range of built-in datatypes when combined with the type modifiers:

DATA TYPE	SIZE (IN BYTES)	RANGE
short int	2	-32,768 to 32,767
unsigned short int	2	0 to 65,535
unsigned int	4	0 to 4,294,967,295
int	4	-2,147,483,648 to 2,147,483,647
long int	4	-2,147,483,648 to 2,147,483,647
unsigned long int	4	0 to 4,294,967,295
long long int	8	$-(2^{63})$ to $(2^{63})-1$
unsigned long long int	8	0 to 18,446,744,073,709,551,615
signed char	1	-128 to 127
unsigned char	1	0 to 255
float	4	
double	8	
long double	12	
wchar_t	2 or 4	1 wide character

We can display the size of all the data types by using the sizeof() function and passing the keyword of the datatype as argument to this function as shown below:

```cpp
// C++ program to sizes of data types

#include<iostream>

using namespace std;


int main()
{
    cout << "Size of char : " << sizeof(char)
        << " byte" << endl;
    cout << "Size of int : " << sizeof(int)
        << " bytes" << endl;
    cout << "Size of short int : " << sizeof(short int)
        << " bytes" << endl;
    cout << "Size of long int : " << sizeof(long int)
        << " bytes" << endl;
    cout << "Size of signed long int : " << sizeof(signed long int)
        << " bytes" << endl;
    cout << "Size of unsigned long int : " << sizeof(unsigned long int)
```

```
            << " bytes" << endl;
    cout << "Size of float : " << sizeof(float)
        << " bytes" <<endl;
    cout << "Size of double : " << sizeof(double)
        << " bytes" << endl;
    cout << "Size of wchar_t : " << sizeof(wchar_t)
        << " bytes" <<endl;


    return 0;
}
```

Output:

```
Size of char : 1 byte

Size of int : 4 bytes

Size of short int : 2 bytes

Size of long int : 8 bytes

Size of signed long int : 8 bytes

Size of unsigned long int : 8 bytes

Size of float : 4 bytes

Size of double : 8 bytes

Size of wchar_t : 4 bytes
```

C++ Variable Types

A variable provides us with named storage that our programs can manipulate. Each variable in C++ has a specific type, which determines the size and layout of the variable's memory; the range of values that can be stored within that memory; and the set of operations that can be applied to the variable.

The name of a variable can be composed of letters, digits, and the underscore character. It must begin with either a letter or an underscore. Upper and lowercase letters are distinct because C++ is case-sensitive.

There are following basic types of variable in C++:

Sr. No.	Type & Description
1	bool Stores either value true or false.

2	char
	Typically a single octet (one byte). This is an integer type.
3	int
	The most natural size of integer for the machine.
4	float
	A single-precision floating point value.
5	double
	A double-precision floating point value.
6	void
	Represents the absence of type.
7	wchar_t
	A wide character type.

Variable Definition in C++

A variable definition tells the compiler where and how much storage to create for the variable. A variable definition specifies a data type, and contains a list of one or more variables of that type as follows:

```
type variable_list;
```

Here, type must be a valid C++ data type including char, w_char, int, float, double, bool or any user-defined object, etc., and variable_list may consist of one or more identifier names separated by commas. Some valid declarations are shown here:

```
int i, j, k;

char c, ch;

float f, salary;

double d;
```

The line int i, j, k; both declares and defines the variables i, j and k; which instructs the compiler to create variables named i, j and k of type int.

Variables can be initialized (assigned an initial value) in their declaration. The initializer consists of an equal sign followed by a constant expression as follows:

```
type variable_name = value;
```

Some examples are:

```
extern int d = 3, f = 5; // declaration of d and f.

int d = 3, f = 5; // definition and initializing d and f.

byte z = 22; // definition and initializes z.

char x = 'x'; // the variable x has the value 'x'.
```

For definition without an initializer: variables with static storage duration are implicitly initialized with NULL (all bytes have the value 0); the initial value of all other variables is undefined.

Variable Declaration in C++

A variable declaration provides assurance to the compiler that there is one variable existing with the given type and name so that compiler proceed for further compilation without needing complete detail about the variable. A variable declaration has its meaning at the time of compilation only, compiler needs actual variable definition at the time of linking of the program.

A variable declaration is useful when you are using multiple files and you define your variable in one of the files which will be available at the time of linking of the program. You will use extern keyword to declare a variable at any place. Though you can declare a variable multiple times in your C++ program, but it can be defined only once in a file, a function or a block of code.

Example: Try the following example where a variable has been declared at the top, but it has been defined inside the main function:

```cpp
#include <iostream>

using namespace std;

// Variable declaration:

extern int a, b;

extern int c;

extern float f;


int main () {

  // Variable definition:

  int a, b;

  int c;

  float f;


  // actual initialization

  a = 10;

  b = 20;

  c = a + b;


  cout << c << endl ;

  f = 70.0/3.0;
```

```
cout << f << endl ;


 return 0;

}
```

When the above code is compiled and executed, it produces the following result:

30

23.3333

Same concept applies on function declaration where you provide a function name at the time of its declaration and its actual definition can be given anywhere else. For example:

```
// function declaration

int func();

int main() {

 // function call

 int i = func();

}

// function definition

int func() {

 return 0;

}
```

Lvalues and Rvalues

There are two kinds of expressions in C++:

- Lvalue: Expressions that refer to a memory location is called "lvalue" expression. An lvalue may appear as either the left-hand or right-hand side of an assignment.

- Rvalue: The term rvalue refers to a data value that is stored at some address in memory. An rvalue is an expression that cannot have a value assigned to it which means an rvalue may appear on the right- but not left-hand side of an assignment.

Variables are lvalues and so may appear on the left-hand side of an assignment. Numeric literals are rvalues and so may not be assigned and cannot appear on the left-hand side. Following is a valid statement:

```
int g = 20;
```

But the following is not a valid statement and would generate compile-time error:

```
10 = 20;
```

C++ Loop Types

There may be a situation, when you need to execute a block of code several numbers of times. In general, statements are executed sequentially: The first statement in a function is executed first, followed by the second, and so on.

Programming languages provide various control structures that allow for more complicated execution paths.

A loop statement allows us to execute a statement or group of statements multiple times and following is the general from of a loop statement in most of the programming languages:

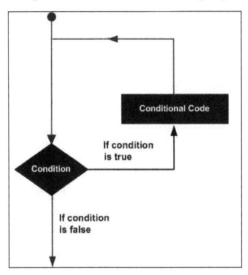

C++ programming language provides the following type of loops to handle looping requirements:

Sr. No.	Loop Type and Description
1	while loop Repeats a statement or group of statements while a given condition is true. It tests the condition before executing the loop body.
2	for loop Execute a sequence of statements multiple times and abbreviates the code that manages the loop variable.
3	do...while loop Like a 'while' statement, except that it tests the condition at the end of the loop body.
4	nested loops You can use one or more loop inside any another 'while', 'for' or 'do..while' loop.

Loop Control Statements

Loop control statements change execution from its normal sequence. When execution leaves a scope, all automatic objects that were created in that scope are destroyed.

C++ supports the following control statements:

Sr. No.	Control Statement and Description
1	break statement Terminates the loop or switch statement and transfers execution to the statement immediately following the loop or switch.
2	continue statement Causes the loop to skip the remainder of its body and immediately retest its condition prior to reiterating.
3	goto statement Transfers control to the labeled statement. Though it is not advised to use goto statement in your program.

The Infinite Loop

A loop becomes infinite loop if a condition never becomes false. The for loop is traditionally used for this purpose. Since none of the three expressions that form the 'for' loop are required, you can make an endless loop by leaving the conditional expression empty.

```
#include <iostream>

using namespace std;


int main () {

 for( ; ; ) {

 printf("This loop will run forever.\n");

 }

 return 0;

}
```

When the conditional expression is absent, it is assumed to be true. You may have an initialization and increment expression, but C++ programmers more commonly use the 'for (;;)' construct to signify an infinite loop.

C++ Functions

A function is a set of statements that take inputs, do some specific computation and produces output. The idea is to put some commonly or repeatedly done task together and make a function so that instead of writing the same code again and again for different inputs, we can call the function.

Example: Here is a simple C++ program to demonstrate functions.

```c
#include <stdio.h>

// An example function that takes two parameters 'x' and 'y'
// as input and returns max of two input numbers
int max(int x, int y)
{
    if (x > y)
      return x;
    else
      return y;
}


// main function that doesn't receive any parameter and
// returns integer.
int main(void)
{
    int a = 10, b = 20;

    // Calling above function to find max of 'a' and 'b'
    int m = max(a, b);

    printf("m is %d", m);
    return 0;
}
```

Output: m is 20.

The Need of Functions

- Functions help us in reducing code redundancy. If functionality is performed at multiple places in software, then rather than writing the same code, again and again, we create a function and call it everywhere. This also helps in maintenance as we have to change at one place if we make future changes to the functionality.

- Functions make code modular. Consider a big file having many lines of codes. It becomes really simple to read and use the code if the code is divided into functions.

- Functions provide abstraction. For example, we can use library functions without worrying about their internal working.

Function Declaration

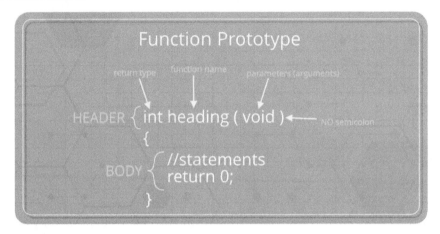

A function declaration tells the compiler about the number of parameters function takes data-types of parameters and return type of function. Putting parameter names in function declaration is optional in the function declaration, but it is necessary to put them in the definition. Below are examples of function declarations.

```
// A function that takes two integers as parameters

// and returns an integer

int max(int, int);
```

```
// A function that takes a int pointer and an int variable as parameters

// and returns an pointer of type int

int *swap(int*,int);
```

```
// A function that takes a charas parameters

// and returns an reference variable

char *call(char b);
```

```
// A function that takes a char and an int as parameters

// and returns an integer

int fun(char, int);
```

It is always recommended to declare a function before it is used.

Parameter Passing to Functions

The parameters passed to function are called actual parameters. For example, in the above program 10 and 20 are actual parameters.

The parameters received by function are called formal parameters. For example, in the above program x and y are formal parameters.

There are two most popular ways to pass parameters:

- Pass by Value: In this parameter passing method, values of actual parameters are copied to function's formal parameters and the two types of parameters are stored in different memory locations. So any changes made inside functions are not reflected in actual parameters of caller.

- Pass by Reference: Both actual and formal parameters refer to same locations, so any changes made inside the function are actually reflected in actual parameters of caller.

In C, parameters are always passed by value. Parameters are always passed by value in C. For example in the below code, value of x is not modified using the function fun().

```c
#include <stdio.h>

void fun(int x)

{

   x = 30;

}


int main(void)

{

    int x = 20;

    fun(x);

    printf("x = %d", x);

    return 0;

}
```

Output:

```
x = 20.
```

However, in C, we can use pointers to get the effect of pass by reference. For example, consider the below program. The function fun() expects a pointer ptr to an integer (or an address of an integer). It modifies the value at the address ptr. The dereference operator * is used to access the value at an address. In the statement '*ptr = 30', value at address ptr is changed to 30. The address operator & is used to get the address of a variable of any data type. In the function call statement 'fun(&x)', the address of x is passed so that x can be modified using its address.

```c
#include <stdio.h>

void fun(int x)

{
```

```
    x = 30;
}


int main(void)
{
    int x = 20;
    fun(x);
    printf("x = %d", x);
    return 0;
}
```

Output:

```
x = 30
```

C++ Decision Making Statements

Decision making is about deciding the order of execution of statements based on certain conditions or repeat a group of statements until certain specified conditions are met. C++ handles decision-making by supporting the following statements:

- *if* statement.
- *switch* statement.
- conditional operator statement.
- *goto* statement.

Decision Making with if Statement

The if statement may be implemented in different forms depending on the complexity of conditions to be tested. The different forms are:

- Simple *if* statement.
- *if....else* statement.
- Nested *if....else* statement.
- *else if* statement.

Simple if Statement

The general form of a simple *if* statement is,

```
if(expression)

{

    statement-inside;

}

    statement-outside;
```

If the expression is true, then 'statement-inside' will be executed, otherwise 'statement-inside' is skipped and only 'statement-outside' will be executed.

Example:

```
#include< iostream.h>

int main( )

{

    int x,y;

    x=15;

    y=13;

    if (x > y )

    {

        cout << "x is greater than y";

    }

}
```

Output:

```
x is greater than y.
```

if...else Statement

The general form of a simple *if...else* statement is,

```
if(expression)

{

    statement-block1;

}

else

{

    statement-block2;

}
```

If the 'expression' is true or returns true, then the 'statement-block1' will get executed, else 'statement-block1' will be skipped and 'statement-block2' will be executed.

Example:

```
void main( )

{

    int x,y;

    x=15;

    y=18;

    if (x > y )

    {

        cout << "x is greater than y";

    }

    else

    {

        cout << "y is greater than x";

    }

}
```

Output:

```
y is greater than x.
```

Nested if....else Statement

The general form of a nested *if...else* statement is,

```
if(expression)

{

    if(expression1)

    {

        statement-block1;

    }

    else

    {

        statement-block2;

    }
```

```
}

else

{

    statement-block3;

}
```

if 'expression' is false or returns false, then the 'statement-block3' will be executed, otherwise execution will enter the if condition and check for 'expression 1'. Then if the 'expression 1' is true or returns true, then the 'statement-block1' will be executed otherwise 'statement-block2' will be executed.

Example:

```
void main( )

{

    int a,b,c;

    cout << "enter 3 number";

    cin >> a >> b >> c;

    if(a > b)

    {

        if( a > c)

        {

            cout << "a is greatest";

        }

        else

        {

            cout << "c is greatest";

        }

    }

    else

    {

        if( b> c)

        {

            cout << "b is greatest";

        }

        else
```

```
        {
                cout << "c is greatest";

        }

    }

}
```

else-if Ladder

The general form of *else-if* ladder is,

```
if(expression 1)

{

    statement-block1;

}
else if(expression 2)

{

    statement-block2;

}
else if(expression 3 )

{

    statement-block3;

}
else

    default-statement;
```

The expression is tested from the top(of the ladder) downwards. As soon as the true condition is found, the statement associated with it is executed.

Example:

```
void main( )

{

    int a;

    cout << "enter a number";

    cin >> a;

    if( a%5==0 && a%8==0)

    {

        cout << "divisible by both 5 and 8";
```

```
    }

    else if ( a%8==0 )

    {

        cout << "divisible by 8";

    }

    else if(a%5==0)

    {

        cout << "divisible by 5";

    }

    else

    {

        cout << "divisible by none";

    }

}
```

If you enter value 40 for the variable a, then the output will be:

Output: divisible by both 5 and 8.

C++ Arrays

An array is a series of elements of the same type placed in contiguous memory locations that can be individually referenced by adding an index to a unique identifier.

That means that, for example, five values of type int can be declared as an array without having to declare 5 different variables (each with its own identifier). Instead, using an array, the five int values are stored in contiguous memory locations, and all five can be accessed using the same identifier, with the proper index.

For example, an array containing 5 integer values of type int called foo could be represented as:

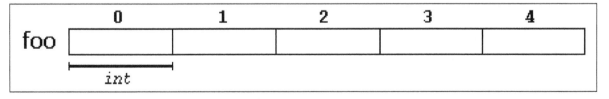

where each blank panel represents an element of the array. In this case, these are values of type int. These elements are numbered from 0 to 4, being 0 the first and 4 the last; In C++, the first element in an array is always numbered with a zero (not a one), no matter its length.

Like a regular variable, an array must be declared before it is used. A typical declaration for an array in C++ is:

```
type name [elements];
```

where type is a valid type (such as int, float...), name is a valid identifier and the elements field (which is always enclosed in square brackets []), specifies the length of the array in terms of the number of elements.

Therefore, the foo array, with five elements of type int, can be declared as:

```
int foo [5];
```

The elements field within square brackets [], representing the number of elements in the array, must be a constant expression, since arrays are blocks of static memory whose size must be determined at compile time, before the program runs.

Initializing Arrays

By default, regular arrays of local scope (for example, those declared within a function) are left uninitialized. This means that none of its elements are set to any particular value; their contents are undetermined at the point the array is declared.

But the elements in an array can be explicitly initialized to specific values when it is declared, by enclosing those initial values in braces {}. For example:

```
int foo [5] = { 16, 2, 77, 40, 12071 };
```

This statement declares an array that can be represented like this:

	0	1	2	3	4
foo	16	2	77	40	12071

int

The number of values between braces {} shall not be greater than the number of elements in the array. For example, in the example above, foo was declared having 5 elements (as specified by the number enclosed in square brackets, []), and the braces {} contained exactly 5 values, one for each element. If declared with less, the remaining elements are set to their default values (which for fundamental types, means they are filled with zeroes). For example:

```
int bar [5] = { 10, 20, 30 };
```

Will create an array like this:

	0	1	2	3	4
bar	10	20	30	0	0

int

The initializer can even have no values, just the braces:

```
int baz [5] = { };
```

This creates an array of five int values, each initialized with a value of zero:

	0	1	2	3	4
baz	0	0	0	0	0

int

When an initialization of values is provided for an array, C++ allows the possibility of leaving the square brackets empty []. In this case, the compiler will assume automatically a size for the array that matches the number of values included between the braces {}:

```
int foo [] = { 16, 2, 77, 40, 12071 };
```

After this declaration, array foo would be 5 int long, since we have provided 5 initialization values.

Finally, the evolution of C++ has led to the adoption of *universal initialization* also for arrays. Therefore, there is no longer need for the equal sign between the declaration and the initializer. Both these statements are equivalent:

```
int foo[] = { 10, 20, 30 };
```

```
int foo[] { 10, 20, 30 };
```

Static arrays, and those declared directly in a namespace (outside any function), are always initialized. If no explicit initializer is specified, all the elements are default-initialized (with zeroes, for fundamental types).

Accessing the Values of an Array

The values of any of the elements in an array can be accessed just like the value of a regular variable of the same type. The syntax is:

```
name[index]
```

Following the previous examples in which `foo` had 5 elements and each of those elements was of type `int`, the name which can be used to refer to each element is the following:

	foo[0]	foo[1]	foo[2]	foo[3]	foo[4]
foo					

For example, the following statement stores the value 75 in the third element of foo:

```
foo [2] = 75;
```

and, for example, the following copies the value of the third element of foo to a variable called x:

```
x = foo[2];
```

Therefore, the expression `foo` is itself a variable of type int.

Notice that the third element of `foo` is specified `foo`, since the first one is `foo`, the second one is foo, and therefore, the third one is `foo`. By this same reason, its last element is `foo`. Therefore, if we write `foo`, we would be accessing the sixth element of `foo`, and therefore actually exceeding the size of the array.

In C++, it is syntactically correct to exceed the valid range of indices for an array. This can create problems, since accessing out-of-range elements do not cause errors on compilation, but can cause errors on runtime.

At this point, it is important to be able to clearly distinguish between the two uses that brackets [] have related to arrays. They perform two different tasks: one is to specify the size of arrays when they are declared; and the second one is to specify indices for concrete array elements when they are accessed. Do not confuse these two possible uses of brackets [] with arrays.

```cpp
int foo[5];           // declaration of a new array

foo[2] = 75;          // access to an element of the array.
```

The main difference is that the declaration is preceded by the type of the elements, while the access is not.

Some other valid operations with arrays:

```cpp
foo[0] = a;

foo[a] = 75;

b = foo [a+2];

foo[foo[a]] = foo[2] + 5;
```

For example:

```cpp
// arrays example

#include <iostream>

using namespace std;


int foo [] = {16, 2, 77, 40, 12071};

int n, result=0;


int main ()

{

   for ( n=0 ; n<5 ; ++n )

   {

     result += foo[n];
```

```
    }

    cout << result;

    return 0;

}
```

Multidimensional Arrays

Multidimensional arrays can be described as "arrays of arrays". For example, a bidimensional array can be imagined as a two-dimensional table made of elements, all of them of a same uniform data type.

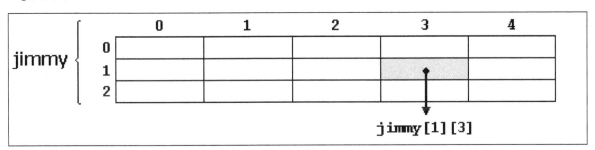

Jimmy represents a bidimensional array of 3 per 5 elements of type `int`. The C++ syntax for this is:

```
int jimmy ;[3][5];
```

and, for example, the way to reference the second element vertically and fourth horizontally in an expression would be:

```
jimmy[1][3]
```

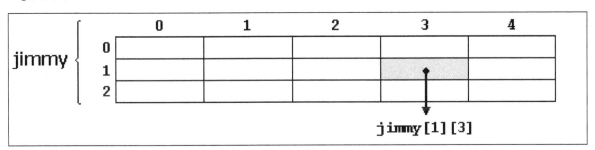

(remember that array indices always begin with zero).

Multidimensional arrays are not limited to two indices (i.e., two dimensions). They can contain as many indices as needed. Although be careful: the amount of memory needed for an array increases exponentially with each dimension. For example:

```
char century [100][365][24][60][60];
```

declares an array with an element of type char for each second in a century. This amounts to more than 3 billion char. So this declaration would consume more than 3 gigabytes of memory.

At the end, multidimensional arrays are just an abstraction for programmers, since the same results can be achieved with a simple array, by multiplying its indices:

```
int jimmy [3][5];    // is equivalent to
```

```
int jimmy [15];      // (3 * 5 = 15)
```

With the only difference that with multidimensional arrays; the compiler automatically remembers the depth of each imaginary dimension. The following two pieces of code produce the exact same result, but one uses a bidimensional array while the other uses a simple array:

Multidimensional Array	Pseudo-multidimensional Array
```#define WIDTH 5```	```#define WIDTH 5```
```#define HEIGHT 3```	```#define HEIGHT 3```
```int jimmy [HEIGHT][WIDTH];``` ```int n,m;```	```int jimmy [HEIGHT * WIDTH];``` ```int n,m;```
```int main ()``` ```{```	```int main ()``` ```{```

``` for (n=0; n<HEIGHT; n++)```
```   for (m=0; m<WIDTH; m++)```
```   {```
```   jimmy[n][m]=(n+1)*(m+1);```
```   }```
```}```
	``` for (n=0; n<HEIGHT; n++)```
	``` for (m=0; m<WIDTH; m++)```
	``` {```
	``` jimmy[n*WIDTH+m]=(n+1)*(m+1);```
	``` }```
	```}```

None of the two code snippets above produce any output on the screen, but both assign values to the memory block called jimmy in the following way:

		0	1	2	3	4
jimmy	0	1	2	3	4	5
	1	2	4	6	8	10
	2	3	6	9	12	15

The code uses defined constants for the width and height, instead of using directly their numerical values. This gives the code a better readability, and allows changes in the code to be made easily in one place.

Arrays as Parameters

At some point, we may need to pass an array to a function as a parameter. In C++, it is not possible to pass the entire block of memory represented by an array to a function directly as an argument. But what can be passed instead is its address. In practice, this has almost the same effect, and it is a much faster and more efficient operation.

To accept an array as parameter for a function, the parameters can be declared as the array type, but with empty brackets, omitting the actual size of the array. For example:

```
void procedure (int arg[])
```

This function accepts a parameter of type "`array of int`" called `arg`. In order to pass to this function an array declared as:

```
int myarray ;
```

It would be enough to write a call like this:

```
procedure (myarray);
```

Here you have a complete example:

``c++
// arrays as parameters
 	
#include <iostream>
 	
using namespace std;
 	
void printarray (int arg[], int length) {
 	
  for (int n=0; n<length; ++n)
 	
    cout << arg[n] << ' ';
 	
  cout << '\n';
 	
}
 	
int main ()
 	
{
 	
  int firstarray[] = {5, 10, 15};
 	
  int secondarray[] = {2, 4, 6, 8, 10};
 	
  printarray (firstarray,3);
 	
  printarray (secondarray,5);
 	
}```
	``5 10 15
	
	2 4 6 8 10```

In the code above, the first parameter (int arg[]) accepts any array whose elements are of type int, whatever its length. For that reason, we have included a second parameter that tells the function the length of each array that we pass to it as its first parameter. This allows the for loop that prints out the array to know the range to iterate in the array passed, without going out of range. In a function declaration, it is also possible to include multidimensional arrays. The format for a tridimensional array parameter is:

```
base_type[][depth][depth]
```

For example, a function with a multidimensional array as argument could be:

```
void procedure (int myarray[])
```

Notice that the first brackets [] are left empty, while the following ones specify sizes for their respective dimensions. This is necessary in order for the compiler to be able to determine the depth of each additional dimension.

In a way, passing an array as argument always loses a dimension. The reason behind is that, for historical reasons, arrays cannot be directly copied, and thus what is really passed is a pointer.

Library Arrays

The arrays explained above are directly implemented as a language feature, inherited from the C language. They are a great feature, but by restricting its copy and easily decay into pointers, they probably suffer from an excess of optimization.

To overcome some of these issues with language built-in arrays, C++ provides an alternative array type as a standard container. It is a type template (a class template, in fact) defined in header <array>.

Just as an example, these are two versions of the same example using the language built-in array described here and the container in the library:

Language built-in array	Container library array
```#include <iostream>```	```#include <iostream>```
	```#include <array>```
```using namespace std;```	```using namespace std;```
```int main()```	```int main()```
```{```	```{```
``` int myarray[3] = {10,20,30};```	``` array<int,3> myarray {10,20,30};```
``` for (int i=0; i<3; ++i)```	``` for (int i=0; i<myarray.size(); ++i)```
``` ++myarray[i];```	``` ++myarray[i];```
``` for (int elem : myarray)```	``` for (int elem : myarray)```
``` cout << elem << '\n';```	``` cout << elem << '\n';```
```}```	```}```

As you can see, both kinds of arrays use the same syntax to access its elements: `myarray[i]`. Other than that, the main differences lay on the declaration of the array, and the inclusion of an additional header for the library array. Notice also how it is easy to access the size of the library array.

C++ Strings

Strings are used for storing text.

A `string` variable contains a collection of characters surrounded by double quotes.

Example: Create a variable of type string and assign it a value.

```
string greeting = "Hello";
```

To use strings, you must include an additional header file in the source code, the `<string>` library.

Example:

```
// Include the string library
#include <string>


// Create a string variable
string greeting = "Hello";
```

String Concatenation

The + operator can be used between strings to add them together to make a new string. This is called concatenation.

Example:

```
string firstName = "John ";
string lastName = "Doe";
string fullName = firstName + lastName;
cout << fullName;
```

String Length

A string in C++ is actually an object, which contain functions that can perform certain operations on strings. For example, the length of a string can be found with the `length()`function.

Example:

```
string txt = "ABCDEFGHIJKLMNOPQRSTUVWXYZ";
cout << "The length of the txt string is: " << txt.length();
```

Access Strings

You can access the characters in a string by referring to its index number inside square brackets [].

This example prints the first character in myString.

Example:

```
string myString = "Hello";

cout << myString[0];

// Outputs H
```

This example prints the second character in myString.

Example:

```
string myString = "Hello";

cout << myString[1];

// Outputs e
```

Change String Characters

To change the value of a specific character in a string, refer to the index number, and use single quotes.

Example:

```
string myString = "Hello";

myString[0] = 'J';

cout << myString;

// Outputs Jello instead of Hello
```

User Input Strings

It is possible to use the extraction operator >> on cin to display a string entered by a user.

Example:

```
string firstName;
cout << "Type your first name: ";
cin >> firstName; // get user input from the keyboard
cout << "Your name is: " << firstName;


// Type your first name: John
// Your name is: John
```

However, `cin` considers a space (whitespace, tabs, etc) as a terminating character, which means that it can only display a single word (even if you type many words).

Example:

```
string fullName;

cout << "Type your full name: ";

cin >> fullName;

cout << "Your name is: " << fullName;



// Type your full name: John Doe

// Your name is: John
```

From the example above, you would expect the program to print "John Doe", but it only prints "John".

That's why, when working with strings, we often use the `getline()` function to read a line of text. It takes `cin` as the first parameter, and the string variable as second.

Example:

```
string fullName;

cout << "Type your full name: ";

getline (cin, fullName);

cout << "Your name is: " << fullName;



// Type your full name: John Doe

// Your name is: John Doe
```

Adding Numbers and Strings

If you add two numbers, the result will be a number.

Example:

```
int x = 10;

int y = 20;

int z = x + y;       // z will be 30 (an integer)
```

If you add two strings, the result will be a string concatenation.

Example:

```
string x = "10";
```

```
string y = "20";

string z = x + y;    // z will be 1020 (a string)
```

If you try to add a number to a string, an error occurs.

Example:

```
string x = "10";

int y = 20;

string z = x + y;
```

Omitting Namespace

You might see some C++ programs that run without the standard namespace library. The using namespace std line can be omitted and replaced with the std keyword, followed by the : : operator for string (and cout) objects:

Example:

```
#include <iostream>

#include <string>


int main() {

  std::string greeting = "Hello";

  std::cout << greeting;

  return 0;

}
```

C++ Pointers

The pointer in C++ language is a variable, it is also known as locator or indicator that points to an address of a value.

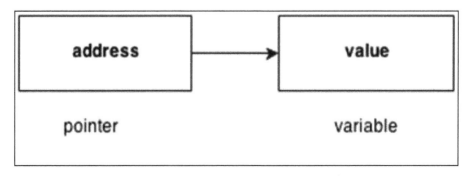

Advantage of Pointer

- Pointer reduces the code and improves the performance, it is used to retrieving strings, trees etc. and used with arrays, structures and functions.

- We can return multiple values from function using pointer.

- It makes you able to access any memory location in the computer's memory.

Usage of Pointer

There are many usage of pointers in C++ language:

- Dynamic memory allocation: In c language, we can dynamically allocate memory using malloc() and calloc() functions where pointer is used.

- Arrays, Functions and Structures: Pointers in c language are widely used in arrays, functions and structures. It reduces the code and improves the performance.

Symbols used in Pointer

Symbol	Name	Description
& (ampersand sign)	Address operator	Determine the address of a variable.
* (asterisk sign)	Indirection operator	Access the value of an address.

Declaring a Pointer

The pointer in C++ language can be declared using * (asterisk symbol).

```
int *   a; //pointer to int

char *  c; //pointer to char
```

Pointer Example

Let's see the simple example of using pointers printing the address and value.

```
#include <iostream>

using namespace std;

int main()

{

int number=30;

int *  p;

p=&number;//stores the address of number variable

cout<<"Address of number variable is:"<<&number<<endl;

cout<<"Address of p variable is:"<<p<<endl;
```

```
cout<<"Value of p variable is:"<<*p<<endl;

    return 0;

}
```

Output:

```
Address of number variable is:0x7ffccc8724c4

Address of p variable is:0x7ffccc8724c4

Value of p variable is:30
```

Pointer Program to Swap 2 Numbers without using 3rd Variable

```
#include <iostream>

using namespace std;

int main()

{

int a=20,b=10,*p1=&a,*p2=&b;

cout<<"Before swap: *p1="<<*p1<<" *p2="<<*p2<<endl;

*p1=*p1+*p2;

*p2=*p1-*p2;

*p1=*p1-*p2;

cout<<"After swap: *p1="<<*p1<<" *p2="<<*p2<<endl;

    return 0;

}
```

Output:

```
Before swap: *p1=20 *p2=10

After swap: *p1=10 *p2=20
```

Numbers in C++

Normally, when we work with Numbers, we use primitive data types such as int, short, long, float and double, etc. The number data types, their possible values and number ranges have been explained while discussing C++ Data Types.

Defining Numbers in C++

Here is another consolidated example to define various types of numbers in C++:

```
#include <iostream>
```

```
using namespace std;

int main () {
   // number definition:
   short   s;
   int     i;
   long    l;
   float   f;
   double  d;

   // number assignments;
   s = 10;
   i = 1000;
   l = 1000000;
   f = 230.47;
   d = 30949.374;

   // number printing;
   cout << "short   s :" << s << endl;
   cout << "int     i :" << i << endl;
   cout << "long    l :" << l << endl;
   cout << "float   f :" << f << endl;
   cout << "double d :" << d << endl;

   return 0;
}
```

When the above code is compiled and executed, it produces the following result:

```
short   s :10
int     i :1000
long    l :1000000
float   f :230.47
double d :30949.4
```

Math Operations in C++

In addition to the various functions you can create, C++ also includes some useful functions you can use. These functions are available in standard C and C++ libraries and called built-in functions. These are functions that can be included in your program and then use.

C++ has a rich set of mathematical operations, which can be performed on various numbers. Following table lists down some useful built-in mathematical functions available in C++.

To utilize these functions you need to include the math header file <cmath>.

Sr. No.	Function and Purpose
1	double cos(double); This function takes an angle (as a double) and returns the cosine.
2	double sin(double); This function takes an angle (as a double) and returns the sine.
3	double tan(double); This function takes an angle (as a double) and returns the tangent.
4	double log(double); This function takes a number and returns the natural log of that number.
5	double pow(double, double); The first is a number you wish to raise and the second is the power you wish to raise it t
6	double hypot(double, double); If you pass this function the length of two sides of a right triangle, it will return you the length of the hypotenuse.
7	double sqrt(double); You pass this function a number and it gives you the square root.
8	int abs(int); This function returns the absolute value of an integer that is passed to it.
9	double fabs(double); This function returns the absolute value of any decimal number passed to it.
10	double floor(double); Finds the integer which is less than or equal to the argument passed to it.

Following is a simple example to show few of the mathematical operations:

```
Live Demo

#include <iostream>

#include <cmath>

using namespace std;


int main () {

   // number definition:
```

```
short   s = 10;

int     i = -1000;

long    l = 100000;

float   f = 230.47;

double d = 200.374;


// mathematical operations;

cout << "sin(d)  :" << sin(d) << endl;

cout << "abs(i)  :" << abs(i) << endl;

cout << "floor(d) :" << floor(d) << endl;

cout << "sqrt(f) :" << sqrt(f) << endl;

cout << "pow( d, 2) :" << pow(d, 2) << endl;


    return 0;

}
```

When the above code is compiled and executed, it produces the following result:

```
sign(d)      :-0.634939
abs(i)       :1000
floor(d)     :200
sqrt(f)      :15.1812
pow( d, 2 ) :40149.7
```

Random Numbers in C++

There are many cases where you will wish to generate a random number. There are actually two functions you will need to know about random number generation. The first is rand(), this function will only return a pseudo random number. The way to fix this is to first call the srand() function.

Following is a simple example to generate few random numbers. This example makes use of time() function to get the number of seconds on your system time, to randomly seed the rand() function:

```
#include <iostream>

#include <ctime>

#include <cstdlib>


using namespace std;
```

```
int main () {
   int i,j;

   // set the seed
   srand( (unsigned)time( NULL ) );

   /* generate 10  random numbers. */
   for( i = 0; i < 10; i++ ) {
      // generate actual random number
      j = rand();
      cout <<" Random Number : " << j << endl;
   }

   return 0;
}
```

When the above code is compiled and executed, it produces the following result:

```
Random Number : 1748144778

Random Number : 630873888

Random Number : 2134540646

Random Number : 219404170

Random Number : 902129458

Random Number : 920445370

Random Number : 1319072661

Random Number : 257938873

Random Number : 1256201101

Random Number : 580322989
```

C++ Files and Streams

This requires another standard C++ library called fstream, which defines three new data types:

Sr. No.	Data Type and Description
1	ofstream This data type represents the output file stream and is used to create files and to write information to files.

2	ifstream
	This data type represents the input file stream and is used to read information from files.
3	fstream
	This data type represents the file stream generally, and has the capabilities of both ofstream and ifstream which means it can create files, write information to files, and read information from files.

To perform file processing in C++, header files <iostream> and <fstream> must be included in your C++ source file.

Opening a File

A file must be opened before you can read from it or write to it. Either ofstream or fstream object may be used to open a file for writing. And ifstream object is used to open a file for reading purpose only.

Following is the standard syntax for open() function, which is a member of fstream, ifstream, and ofstream objects.

```
void open(const char *filename, ios::openmode mode);
```

Here, the first argument specifies the name and location of the file to be opened and the second argument of the open() member function defines the mode in which the file should be opened.

Sr. No.	Mode Flag and Description
1	`ios::app`
	Append mode. All output to that file to be appended to the end.
2	`ios::ate`
	Open a file for output and move the read/write control to the end of the file.
3	`ios::in`
	Open a file for reading.
4	`ios::out`
	Open a file for writing.
5	`ios::trunc`
	If the file already exists, its contents will be truncated before opening the file.

You can combine two or more of these value by ORing them together. For example if you want to open a file in write mode and want to truncate it in case that already exists, following will be the syntax:

```
ofstream outfile;

outfile.open("file.dat", ios::out | ios::trunc );
```

Similar way, you can open a file for reading and writing purpose as follows:

```
fstream afile;

afile.open("file.dat", ios::out | ios::in );
```

Closing a File

When a C++ program terminates it automatically flushes all the streams, release all the allocated memory and close all the opened files. But it is always a good practice that a programmer should close all the opened files before program termination.

Following is the standard syntax for close () function, which is a member of `fstream`, `ifstream`, and of stream objects.

```
void close();
```

Writing to a File

While doing C++ programming, you write information to a file from your program using the stream insertion operator (<<) just as you use that operator to output information to the screen. The only difference is that you use an `ofstream` or `fstream` object instead of the `cout` object.

Reading from a File

You read information from a file into your program using the stream extraction operator (>>) just as you use that operator to input information from the keyboard. The only difference is that you use an `ifstream` or `fstream` object instead of the `cin` object.

Read and Write Example

Following is the C++ program which opens a file in reading and writing mode. After writing information entered by the user to a file named afile.dat, the program reads information from the file and outputs it onto the screen:

```
#include <fstream>

#include <iostream>

using namespace std;


int main () {

   char data[100];


   // open a file in write mode.

   ofstream outfile;

   outfile.open("afile.dat");


   cout << "Writing to the file" << endl;

   cout << "Enter your name: ";

   cin.getline(data, 100);
```

```
// write inputted data into the file.
outfile << data << endl;

cout << "Enter your age: ";
cin >> data;
cin.ignore();

// again write inputted data into the file.
outfile << data << endl;

// close the opened file.
outfile.close();

// open a file in read mode.
ifstream infile;
infile.open("afile.dat");

cout << "Reading from the file" << endl;
infile >> data;

// write the data at the screen.
cout << data << endl;

// again read the data from the file and display it.
infile >> data;
cout << data << endl;

// close the opened file.
infile.close();

return 0;
}
```

When the above code is compiled and executed, it produces the following sample input and output:

```
$ ./a.out
```

```
Writing to the file

Enter your name: Zara

Enter your age: 9

Reading from the file

Zara

9
```

Above examples make use of additional functions from cin object, like getline() function to read the line from outside and ignore() function to ignore the extra characters left by previous read statement.

File Position Pointers

Both `istream` and `ostream` provide member functions for repositioning the file-position pointer. These member functions are `seekg` ("seek get") for istream and `seekp` ("seek put") for ostream.

The argument to seekg and seekp normally is a long integer. A second argument can be specified to indicate the seek direction. The seek direction can be `ios::beg` (the default) for positioning relative to the beginning of a stream, `ios::cur` for positioning relative to the current position in a stream or `ios::end` for positioning relative to the end of a stream.

The file-position pointer is an integer value that specifies the location in the file as a number of bytes from the file's starting location. Some examples of positioning the "get" file-position pointer are:

```
// position to the nth byte of fileObject (assumes ios::beg)

fileObject.seekg( n );


// position n bytes forward in fileObject

fileObject.seekg( n, ios::cur );


// position n bytes back from end of fileObject

fileObject.seekg( n, ios::end );


// position at end of fileObject

fileObject.seekg( 0, ios::end );
```

C++ Exception Handling

An exception is a problem that arises during the execution of a program. A C++ exception is a response to an exceptional circumstance that arises while a program is running, such as an attempt to divide by zero.

Exceptions provide a way to transfer control from one part of a program to another. C++ exception handling is built upon three keywords: `try, catch`, and `throw`.

- `throw`: A program throws an exception when a problem shows up. This is done using a `throw` keyword.

- `catch`: A program catches an exception with an exception handler at the place in a program where you want to handle the problem. The `catch` keyword indicates the catching of an exception.

- `try`: A `try` block identifies a block of code for which particular exceptions will be activated. It's followed by one or more catch blocks.

Assuming a block will raise an exception, a method catches an exception using a combination of the `try` and `catch` keywords. A try/catch block is placed around the code that might generate an exception. Code within a try/catch block is referred to as protected code, and the syntax for using try/catch as follows:

```
try {
   // protected code
} catch( ExceptionName e1 ) {
   // catch block
} catch( ExceptionName e2 ) {
   // catch block
} catch( ExceptionName eN ) {
   // catch block
}
```

You can list down multiple `catch` statements to catch different type of exceptions in case your `try` block raises more than one exception in different situations.

Throwing Exceptions

Exceptions can be thrown anywhere within a code block using `throw` statement. The operand of the throw statement determines a type for the exception and can be any expression and the type of the result of the expression determines the type of exception thrown.

Following is an example of throwing an exception when dividing by zero condition occurs:

```
double division(int a, int b) {
   if( b == 0 ) {
      throw "Division by zero condition!";
   }
   return (a/b);
}
```

Catching Exceptions

The `catch` block following the `try` block catches any exception. You can specify what type of exception you want to catch and this is determined by the exception declaration that appears in parentheses following the keyword catch.

```
try {
    // protected code
} catch( ExceptionName e ) {
   // code to handle ExceptionName exception
}
```

Above code will catch an exception of `ExceptionName` type. If you want to specify that a catch block should handle any type of exception that is thrown in a try block, you must put an ellipsis, ..., between the parentheses enclosing the exception declaration as follows:

```
try {
    // protected code
} catch(...) {
   // code to handle any exception
}
```

The following is an example, which throws a division by zero exception and we catch it in catch block:

```
#include <iostream>
using namespace std;

double division(int a, int b) {
    if( b == 0 ) {
        throw "Division by zero condition!";
    }
    return (a/b);
}

int main () {
    int x = 50;
    int y = 0;
    double z = 0;

    try {
```

```
    z = division(x, y);

    cout << z << endl;

} catch (const char* msg) {

  cerr << msg << endl;

}


    return 0;

}
```

Because we are raising an exception of type `const char*`, so while catching this exception, we have to use const char* in catch block. If we compile and run above code, this would produce the following result:

```
Division by zero condition!
```

C++ Standard Exceptions

C++ provides a list of standard exceptions defined in `<exception>` which we can use in our programs. These are arranged in a parent-child class hierarchy shown below:

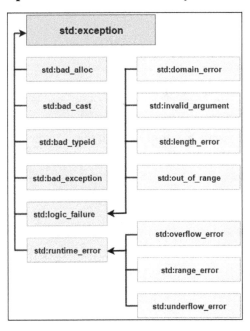

Here is the small description of each exception mentioned in the above hierarchy.

Sr. No	Exception and Description
1	`std::exception` An exception and parent class of all the standard C++ exceptions.
2	`std::bad_alloc` This can be thrown by `new`.

3	`std::bad_cast`
	This can be thrown by dynamic_cast.
4	`std::bad_exception`
	This is useful device to handle unexpected exceptions in a C++ program.
5	`std::bad_typeid`
	This can be thrown by `typeid`.
6	`std::logic_error`
	An exception that theoretically can be detected by reading the code.
7	`std::domain_error`
	This is an exception thrown when a mathematically invalid domain is used.
8	`std::invalid_argument`
	This is thrown due to invalid arguments.
9	`std::length_error`
	This is thrown when a too big std::string is created.
10	`std::out_of_range`
	This can be thrown by the 'at' method, for example a std::vector and std::bitset<>::operator[]().
11	`std::runtime_error`
	An exception that theoretically cannot be detected by reading the code.
12	`std::overflow_error`
	This is thrown if a mathematical overflow occurs.
13	`std::range_error`
	This is occurred when you try to store a value which is out of range.
14	`std::underflow_error`
	This is thrown if a mathematical underflow occurs.

Define New Exceptions

You can define your own exceptions by inheriting and overriding exception class functionality. Following is the example, which shows how you can use std::exception class to implement your own exception in standard way:

```
#include <iostream>

#include <exception>

using namespace std;


struct MyException : public exception {

   const char * what () const throw () {

      return "C++ Exception";
```

```
    }

};


int main() {

    try {

        throw MyException();

    } catch(MyException& e) {

        std::cout << "MyException caught" << std::endl;

        std::cout << e.what() << std::endl;

    } catch(std::exception& e) {

        //Other errors

    }

}
```

This would produce the following result:

```
MyException caught

C++ Exception
```

Here, `what()` is a public method provided by exception class and it has been overridden by all the child exception classes. This returns the cause of an exception.

C++ Dynamic Memory

A good understanding of how dynamic memory really works in C++ is essential to becoming a good C++ programmer. Memory in your C++ program is divided into two parts:

- `The stack`: All variables declared inside the function will take up memory from the stack.

- `The heap`: This is unused memory of the program and can be used to allocate the memory dynamically when program runs.

Many times, you are not aware in advance how much memory you will need to store particular information in a defined variable and the size of required memory can be determined at run time.

You can allocate memory at run time within the heap for the variable of a given type using a special operator in C++ which returns the address of the space allocated. This operator is called `new` operator.

If you are not in need of dynamically allocated memory anymore, you can use `delete` operator, which de-allocates memory that was previously allocated by new operator.

New and Delete Operators

There is following generic syntax to use `new` operator to allocate memory dynamically for any data-type:

```
new data-type;
```

Here, `data-type` could be any built-in data type including an array or any user defined data types include class or structure. Let us start with built-in data types. For example we can define a pointer to type double and then request that the memory be allocated at execution time. We can do this using the `new` operator with the following statements:

```
double* pvalue = NULL; // Pointer initialized with null

pvalue = new double; // Request memory for the variable
```

The memory may not have been allocated successfully, if the free store had been used up. So it is good practice to check if new operator is returning NULL pointer and take appropriate action as below:

```
double* pvalue  = NULL;

if( !(pvalue  = new double )) {

   cout << "Error: out of memory." <<endl;

   exit(1);

}
```

The `malloc()` function from C, still exists in C++, but it is recommended to avoid using malloc() function. The main advantage of new over malloc() is that new doesn't just allocate memory, it constructs objects which is prime purpose of C++.

At any point, when you feel a variable that has been dynamically allocated is not anymore required, you can free up the memory that it occupies in the free store with the 'delete' operator as follows:

```
delete pvalue;          // Release memory pointed to by pvalue
```

Let us put above concepts and form the following example to show how 'new' and 'delete' work:

```
#include <iostream>

using namespace std;


int main () {

   double* pvalue  = NULL; // Pointer initialized with null

   pvalue  = new double;   // Request memory for the variable


   *pvalue = 29494.99;     // Store value at allocated address

   cout << "Value of pvalue : " << *pvalue << endl;
```

```
    delete pvalue;          // free up the memory.


    return 0;

}
```

If we compile and run above code, this would produce the following result:

```
Value of pvalue : 29495
```

Dynamic Memory Allocation for Arrays

Consider you want to allocate memory for an array of characters, i.e., string of 20 characters. Using the same syntax what we have used above we can allocate memory dynamically as shown below:

```
char* pvalue  = NULL;       // Pointer initialized with null

pvalue  = new char[20];     // Request memory for the variable
```

To remove the array that we have just created the statement would look like this:

```
delete [] pvalue;           // Delete array pointed to by pvalue
```

Following the similar generic syntax of new operator, you can allocate for a multi-dimensional array as follows:

```
double** pvalue  = NULL;    // Pointer initialized with null

pvalue  = new double [3][4]; // Allocate memory for a 3x4 array
```

However, the syntax to release the memory for multi-dimensional array will still remain same as above:

```
delete [] pvalue;           // Delete array pointed to by pvalue
```

Dynamic Memory Allocation for Objects

Objects are no different from simple data types. For example, consider the following code where we are going to use an array of objects to clarify the concept:

```
#include <iostream>

using namespace std;


class Box {

    public:

        Box() {

            cout << "Constructor called!" <<endl;
```

```
    }

    ~Box() {

        cout << "Destructor called!" <<endl;

    }

};

int main() {

    Box* myBoxArray = new Box[4];

    delete [] myBoxArray; // Delete array


    return 0;

}
```

If you were to allocate an array of four Box objects, the Simple constructor would be called four times and similarly while deleting these objects, destructor will also be called same number of times.

If we compile and run above code, this would produce the following result:

```
Constructor called!

Constructor called!

Constructor called!

Constructor called!

Destructor called!

Destructor called!

Destructor called!

Destructor called!
```

Namespaces in C++

Consider a situation, when we have two persons with the same name, Zara, in the same class. Whenever we need to differentiate them definitely we would have to use some additional information along with their name, like either the area, if they live in different area or their mother's or father's name, etc.

Same situation can arise in your C++ applications. For example, you might be writing some code that has a function called xyz() and there is another library available which is also having same function xyz(). Now the compiler has no way of knowing which version of xyz() function you are referring to within your code.

A `namespace` is designed to overcome this difficulty and is used as additional information to differentiate similar functions, classes, variables etc. with the same name available in different libraries. Using namespace, you can define the context in which names are defined. In essence, a namespace defines a scope.

Defining a Namespace

A namespace definition begins with the keyword `namespace` followed by the namespace name as follows:

```
namespace namespace_name {

    // code declarations

}
```

To call the namespace-enabled version of either function or variable, prepend `(::)` the namespace name as follows:

```
name::code;  // code could be variable or function.
```

Let us see how namespace scope the entities including variable and functions:

```
Live Demo

#include <iostream>

using namespace std;


// first name space

namespace first_space {

    void func() {

        cout << "Inside first_space" << endl;

    }

}


// second name space

namespace second_space {

    void func() {

        cout << "Inside second_space" << endl;

    }

}
```

```
int main () {

    // Calls function from first name space.

    first_space::func();


    // Calls function from second name space.

    second_space::func();


    return 0;

}
```

If we compile and run above code, this would produce the following result:

```
Inside first_space
```

```
Inside second_space
```

The using Directive

You can also avoid prepending of namespaces with the `using namespace` directive. This directive tells the compiler that the subsequent code is making use of names in the specified namespace. The namespace is thus implied for the following code:

```
#include <iostream>

using namespace std;


// first name space

namespace first_space {

    void func() {

        cout << "Inside first_space" << endl;

    }

}


// second name space

namespace second_space {

    void func() {

        cout << "Inside second_space" << endl;

    }

}
```

```
using namespace first_space;

int main () {

   // This calls function from first name space.

   func();


   return 0;

}
```

If we compile and run above code, this would produce the following result:

```
Inside first_space
```

The 'using' directive can also be used to refer to a particular item within a namespace. For example, if the only part of the std namespace that you intend to use is cout, you can refer to it as follows:

```
using std::cout;
```

Subsequent code can refer to cout without prepending the namespace, but other items in the std namespace will still need to be explicit as follows:

```
#include <iostream>

using std::cout;


int main () {

   cout << "std::endl is used with std!" << std::endl;


   return 0;

}
```

If we compile and run above code, this would produce the following result:

```
std::endl is used with std!
```

Names introduced in a using directive obey normal scope rules. The name is visible from the point of the using directive to the end of the scope in which the directive is found. Entities with the same name defined in an outer scope are hidden.

Discontiguous Namespaces

A namespace can be defined in several parts and so a namespace is made up of the sum of its separately defined parts. The separate parts of a namespace can be spread over multiple files.

So, if one part of the namespace requires a name defined in another file, that name must still be declared. Writing a following namespace definition either defines a new namespace or adds new elements to an existing one:

```
namespace namespace_name {

    // code declarations

}
```

Nested Namespaces

Namespaces can be nested where you can define one namespace inside another name space as follows:

```
namespace namespace_name1 {

    // code declarations

    namespace namespace_name2 {

        // code declarations

    }

}
```

You can access members of nested namespace by using resolution operators as follows:

```
// to access members of namespace_name2

using namespace namespace_name1::namespace_name2;


// to access members of namespace:name1

using namespace namespace_name1;
```

In the above statements if you are using namespace_name1, then it will make elements of name-space_name2 available in the scope as follows:

```
#include <iostream>

using namespace std;


// first name space

namespace first_space {

    void func() {

        cout << "Inside first_space" << endl;

    }


    // second name space
```

```
namespace second_space {

    void func() {

        cout << "Inside second_space" << endl;

    }

  }

}


using namespace first_space::second_space;

int main () {

    // This calls function from second name space.

    func();


    return 0;

}
```

If we compile and run above code, this would produce the following result:

```
Inside second_space
```

C++ Templates

Templates are the foundation of generic programming, which involves writing code in a way that is independent of any particular type. A template is a blueprint or formula for creating a generic class or a function. The library containers like iterators and algorithms are examples of generic programming and have been developed using template concept.

There is a single definition of each container, such as `vector`, but we can define many different kinds of vectors for example, `vector <int>` or `vector <string>`.

You can use templates to define functions as well as classes.

Function Template

The general form of a template function definition is shown here:

```
template <class type> ret-type func-name(parameter list) {

    // body of function

}
```

Here, type is a placeholder name for a data type used by the function. This name can be used within the function definition.

The following is the example of a function template that returns the maximum of two values:

```cpp
#include <iostream>
#include <string>

using namespace std;

template <typename T>
inline T const& Max (T const& a, T const& b) {
    return a < b ? b:a;
}

int main () {
    int i = 39;
    int j = 20;
    cout << "Max(i, j): " << Max(i, j) << endl;

    double f1 = 13.5;
    double f2 = 20.7;
    cout << "Max(f1, f2): " << Max(f1, f2) << endl;

    string s1 = "Hello";
    string s2 = "World";
    cout << "Max(s1, s2): " << Max(s1, s2) << endl;

    return 0;
}
```

If we compile and run above code, this would produce the following result:

```
Max(i, j): 39
Max(f1, f2): 20.7
Max(s1, s2): World
```

Class Template

Just as we can define function templates, we can also define class templates. The general form of a generic class declaration is shown here:

```cpp
template <class type> class class-name {
```

.

.

.

```
}
```

Here, `type` is the placeholder type name, which will be specified when a class is instantiated. You can define more than one generic data type by using a comma-separated list.

Following is the example to define class Stack<> and implement generic methods to push and pop the elements from the stack:

```cpp
#include <iostream>

#include <vector>

#include <cstdlib>

#include <string>

#include <stdexcept>


using namespace std;


template <class T>
class Stack {
    private:
        vector<T> elems;     // elements


    public:
        void push(T const&);  // push element
        void pop();                 // pop element
        T top() const;              // return top element


        bool empty() const {     // return true if empty.
            return elems.empty();
        }
};


template <class T>
void Stack<T>::push (T const& elem) {
    // append copy of passed element
    elems.push_back(elem);
```

```cpp
}


template <class T>
void Stack<T>::pop () {
   if (elems.empty()) {
       throw out_of_range("Stack<>::pop(): empty stack");
   }


   // remove last element
   elems.pop_back();
}


template <class T>
T Stack<T>::top () const {
   if (elems.empty()) {
       throw out_of_range("Stack<>::top(): empty stack");
   }


   // return copy of last element
   return elems.back();
}


int main() {
   try {
       Stack<int>        intStack;  // stack of ints
       Stack<string> stringStack;     // stack of strings


       // manipulate int stack
       intStack.push(7);
       cout << intStack.top() <<endl;


       // manipulate string stack
       stringStack.push("hello");
       cout << stringStack.top() << std::endl;
       stringStack.pop();
```

```
        stringStack.pop();
    } catch (exception const& ex) {
        cerr << "Exception: " << ex.what() <<endl;
        return -1;
    }
}
```

If we compile and run above code, this would produce the following result:

```
7

hello

Exception: Stack<>::pop(): empty stack
```

C++ Preprocessor

The preprocessors are the directives, which give instructions to the compiler to preprocess the information before actual compilation starts.

All preprocessor directives begin with #, and only white-space characters may appear before a preprocessor directive on a line. Preprocessor directives are not C++ statements, so they do not end in a semicolon (;).

There are number of preprocessor directives supported by C++ like #include, #define, #if, #else, #line, etc. Let us see important directives:

The #Define Preprocessor

The #define preprocessor directive creates symbolic constants. The symbolic constant is called a `macro` and the general form of the directive is:

```
#define macro-name replacement-text
```

When this line appears in a file, all subsequent occurrences of macro in that file will be replaced by replacement-text before the program is compiled. For example:

```
#include <iostream>

using namespace std;


#define PI 3.14159


int main () {
```

```
cout << "Value of PI :" << PI << endl;


return 0;

}
```

Now, let us do the preprocessing of this code to see the result assuming we have the source code file. So let us compile it with -E option and redirect the result to test.p. Now, if you check test.p, it will have lots of information and at the bottom, you will find the value replaced as follows:

```
$gcc -E test.cpp > test.p


...

int main () {

    cout << "Value of PI :" << 3.14159 << endl;

    return 0;

}
```

Function-like Macros

You can use #define to define a macro which will take argument as follows:

```
Live Demo

#include <iostream>

using namespace std;


#define MIN(a,b) (((a)<(b)) ? a : b)


int main () {

    int i, j;


    i = 100;

    j = 30;


    cout <<"The minimum is " << MIN(i, j) << endl;


    return 0;
```

```
}
```

If we compile and run above code, this would produce the following result:

```
The minimum is 30
```

Conditional Compilation

There are several directives, which can be used to compile selective portions of your program's source code. This process is called conditional compilation.

The conditional preprocessor construct is much like the 'if' selection structure. Consider the following preprocessor code:

```
#ifndef NULL

    #define NULL 0

#endif
```

You can compile a program for debugging purpose. You can also turn on or off the debugging using a single macro as follows:

```
#ifdef DEBUG

    cerr <<"Variable x = " << x << endl;

#endif
```

This causes the `cerr` statement to be compiled in the program if the symbolic constant DEBUG has been defined before directive #ifdef DEBUG. You can use #if 0 statment to comment out a portion of the program as follows:

```
#if 0

    code prevented from compiling

#endif
```

Let us try the following example:

```
#include <iostream>

using namespace std;

#define DEBUG


#define MIN(a,b)  (((a)<(b)) ? a : b)


int main () {

    int i, j;
```

```
    i = 100;

    j = 30;


#ifdef DEBUG

    cerr <<"Trace: Inside main function" << endl;

#endif


#if 0

    /* This is commented part */

    cout << MKSTR(HELLO C++) << endl;

#endif


    cout <<"The minimum is " << MIN(i, j) << endl;


#ifdef DEBUG

    cerr <<"Trace: Coming out of main function" << endl;

#endif


    return 0;

}
```

If we compile and run above code, this would produce the following result:

```
The minimum is 30

Trace: Inside main function

Trace: Coming out of main function
```

The # and ## Operators

The # and ## preprocessor operators are available in C++ and ANSI/ISO C. The # operator causes a replacement-text token to be converted to a string surrounded by quotes.

Consider the following macro definition:

```
#include <iostream>

using namespace std;


#define MKSTR( x ) #x


int main () {
```

```
cout << MKSTR(HELLO C++) << endl;


    return 0;
}
```

If we compile and run above code, this would produce the following result:

```
HELLO C++
```

Let us see how it worked. It is simple to understand that the C++ preprocessor turns the line:

```
cout << MKSTR(HELLO C++) << endl;
```

Above line will be turned into the following line:

```
cout << "HELLO C++" << endl;
```

The ## operator is used to concatenate two tokens. Here is an example:

```
#define CONCAT( x, y )   x ## y
```

When CONCAT appears in the program, its arguments are concatenated and used to replace the macro. For example, CONCAT(HELLO, C++) is replaced by "HELLO C++" in the program as follows.

```
#include <iostream>

using namespace std;


#define concat(a, b) a ## b

int main() {

    int xy = 100;


    cout << concat(x, y);

    return 0;
}
```

If we compile and run above code, this would produce the following result:

```
100
```

Let us see how it worked. It is simple to understand that the C++ preprocessor transforms:

```
cout << concat(x, y);
```

Above line will be transformed into the following line:

```
cout << xy;
```

Predefined C++ Macros

C++ provides a number of predefined macros mentioned below:

Sr. No.	Macro and Description
1	__LINE__ This contains the current line number of the program when it is being compiled.
2	__FILE__ This contains the current file name of the program when it is being compiled.
3	__DATE__ This contains a string of the form month/day/year that is the date of the translation of the source file into object code.
4	__TIME__ This contains a string of the form hour:minute:second that is the time at which the program was compiled.

Let us see an example for all the above macros:

```
#include <iostream>

using namespace std;


int main () {
    cout << "Value of __LINE__ : " << __LINE__ << endl;
    cout << "Value of __FILE__ : " << __FILE__ << endl;
    cout << "Value of __DATE__ : " << __DATE__ << endl;
    cout << "Value of __TIME__ : " << __TIME__ << endl;


    return 0;
}
```

If we compile and run above code, this would produce the following result:

```
Value of __LINE__ : 6
Value of __FILE__ : test.cpp
Value of __DATE__ : Feb 28 2011
Value of __TIME__ : 18:52:48
```

C++ Signalling Handling

Signals are the interrupts delivered to a process by the operating system which can terminate a program prematurely. You can generate interrupts by pressing Ctrl+C on a UNIX, LINUX, Mac OS X or Windows system.

There are signals which cannot be caught by the program but there is a following list of signals which you can catch in your program and can take appropriate actions based on the signal. These signals are defined in C++ header file <csignal>.

Sr. No.	Signal and Description
1	Sigabrt Abnormal termination of the program, such as a call to `abort`.
2	Sigfpe An erroneous arithmetic operation, such as a divide by zero or an operation resulting in overflow.
3	Sigill Detection of an illegal instruction.
4	Sigint Receipt of an interactive attention signal.
5	Sigsegv An invalid access to storage.
6	Sigterm A termination request sent to the program.

The Signal() Function

C++ signal-handling library provides function `signal` to trap unexpected events. Following is the syntax of the signal() function:

```
void (*signal (int sig, void (*func)(int)))(int);
```

Keeping it simple, this function receives two arguments: first argument as an integer which represents signal number and second argument as a pointer to the signal-handling function.

Let us write a simple C++ program where we will catch SIGINT signal using signal() function. Whatever signal you want to catch in your program, you must register that signal using `signal` function and associate it with a signal handler. Examine the following example:

```cpp
#include <iostream>
#include <csignal>

using namespace std;

void signalHandler( int signum ) {
   cout << "Interrupt signal (" << signum << ") received.\n";

   // cleanup and close up stuff here
   // terminate program
```

```
    exit(signum);
}


int main () {
    // register signal SIGINT and signal handler
    signal(SIGINT, signalHandler);

    while(1) {
        cout << "Going to sleep...." << endl;
        sleep(1);
    }

    return 0;
}
```

When the above code is compiled and executed, it produces the following result:

```
Going to sleep....
Going to sleep....
Going to sleep....
```

Now, press Ctrl+c to interrupt the program and you will see that your program will catch the signal and would come out by printing something as follows:

```
Going to sleep....
Going to sleep....
Going to sleep....
Interrupt signal (2) received.
```

The Raise() Function

You can generate signals by function raise(), which takes an integer signal number as an argument and has the following syntax.

```
int raise (signal sig);
```

Here, sig is the signal number to send any of the signals: SIGINT, SIGABRT, SIGFPE, SIGILL, SIGSEGV, SIGTERM, SIGHUP. Following is the example where we raise a signal internally using raise() function as follows:

```
#include <iostream>
#include <csignal>
```

```cpp
using namespace std;

void signalHandler( int signum ) {
   cout << "Interrupt signal (" << signum << ") received.\n";

   // cleanup and close up stuff here
   // terminate program

   exit(signum);
}


int main () {
   int i = 0;
   // register signal SIGINT and signal handler
   signal(SIGINT, signalHandler);

   while(++i) {
      cout << "Going to sleep...." << endl;
      if( i == 3 ) {
         raise( SIGINT);
      }
      sleep(1);
   }

   return 0;
}
```

When the above code is compiled and executed, it produces the following result and would come out automatically:

```
Going to sleep....
Going to sleep....
Going to sleep....
Interrupt signal (2) received.
```

C++ Multithreading

Multithreading is a specialized form of multitasking and a multitasking is the feature that allows your computer to run two or more programs concurrently. In general, there are two types of multitasking: process-based and thread-based.

Process-based multitasking handles the concurrent execution of programs. Thread-based multitasking deals with the concurrent execution of pieces of the same program.

A multithreaded program contains two or more parts that can run concurrently. Each part of such a program is called a thread, and each thread defines a separate path of execution.

C++ does not contain any built-in support for multithreaded applications. Instead, it relies entirely upon the operating system to provide this feature.

Creating Threads

The following routine is used to create a POSIX thread:

```
#include <pthread.h>

pthread_create (thread, attr, start_routine, arg)
```

Here, `pthread_create` creates a new thread and makes it executable. This routine can be called any number of times from anywhere within your code. Here is the description of the parameters:

Sr. No.	Parameter and Description
1	`thread` An opaque, unique identifier for the new thread returned by the subroutine.
2	`attr` An opaque attribute object that may be used to set thread attributes. You can specify a thread attributes object, or NULL for the default values.
3	`start_routine` The C++ routine that the thread will execute once it is created.
4	`arg` A single argument that may be passed to start_routine. It must be passed by reference as a pointer cast of type void. NULL may be used if no argument is to be passed.

The maximum number of threads that may be created by a process is implementation dependent. Once created, threads are peers, and may create other threads. There is no implied hierarchy or dependency between threads.

Terminating Threads

There is following routine which we use to terminate a POSIX thread:

```
#include <pthread.h>

pthread_exit (status)
```

Here `pthread_exit` is used to explicitly exit a thread. Typically, the pthread_exit() routine is called after a thread has completed its work and is no longer required to exist.

If main() finishes before the threads it has created, and exits with pthread_exit(), the other threads will continue to execute. Otherwise, they will be automatically terminated when main() finishes.

Example: This simple example code creates 5 threads with the pthread_create() routine. Each thread prints a "Hello World!" message, and then terminates with a call to pthread_exit().

```cpp
#include <iostream>

#include <cstdlib>

#include <pthread.h>


using namespace std;


#define NUM_THREADS 5


void *PrintHello(void *threadid) {

    long tid;

    tid = (long)threadid;

    cout << "Hello World! Thread ID, " << tid << endl;

    pthread_exit(NULL);

}


int main () {

    pthread_t threads[NUM_THREADS];

    int rc;

    int i;


    for( i = 0; i < NUM_THREADS; i++ ) {

        cout << "main() : creating thread, " << i << endl;

        rc = pthread_create(&threads[i], NULL, PrintHello, (void *)i);


        if (rc) {

            cout << "Error:unable to create thread," << rc << endl;
```

```
        exit(-1);
      }
   }
   pthread_exit(NULL);
}
```

Compile the following program using -lpthread library as follows:

```
$gcc test.cpp -lpthread
```

Now, execute your program which gives the following output:

```
main() : creating thread, 0
main() : creating thread, 1
main() : creating thread, 2
main() : creating thread, 3
main() : creating thread, 4
Hello World! Thread ID, 0
Hello World! Thread ID, 1
Hello World! Thread ID, 2
Hello World! Thread ID, 3
Hello World! Thread ID, 4
```

Passing Arguments to Threads

This example shows how to pass multiple arguments via a structure. You can pass any data type in a thread callback because it points to void as explained in the following example:

```
#include <iostream>
#include <cstdlib>
#include <pthread.h>


using namespace std;


#define NUM_THREADS 5


struct thread_data {
    int   thread_id;
    char *message;
```

```
};

void *PrintHello(void *threadarg) {
   struct thread_data *my_data;
   my_data = (struct thread_data *) threadarg;

   cout << "Thread ID : " << my_data->thread_id ;
   cout << " Message : " << my_data->message << endl;

   pthread_exit(NULL);
}


int main () {
   pthread_t threads[NUM_THREADS];
   struct thread_data td[NUM_THREADS];
   int rc;
   int i;

   for( i = 0; i < NUM_THREADS; i++ ) {
      cout <<"main() : creating thread, " << i << endl;
      td[i].thread_id = i;
      td[i].message = "This is message";
      rc = pthread_create(&threads[i], NULL, PrintHello, (void *)&td[i]);

      if (rc) {
         cout << "Error:unable to create thread," << rc << endl;
         exit(-1);
      }
   }
   pthread_exit(NULL);
}
```

When the above code is compiled and executed, it produces the following result:

```
main() : creating thread, 0
main() : creating thread, 1
main() : creating thread, 2
```

```
main() : creating thread, 3

main() : creating thread, 4

Thread ID : 3 Message : This is message

Thread ID : 2 Message : This is message

Thread ID : 0 Message : This is message

Thread ID : 1 Message : This is message

Thread ID : 4 Message : This is message
```

Joining and Detaching Threads

There are following two routines which we can use to join or detach threads:

```
pthread_join (threadid, status)
```

```
pthread_detach (threadid)
```

The pthread_join() subroutine blocks the calling thread until the specified 'threadid' thread terminates. When a thread is created, one of its attributes defines whether it is joinable or detached. Only threads that are created as joinable can be joined. If a thread is created as detached, it can never be joined.

This example demonstrates how to wait for thread completions by using the Pthread join routine.

```
#include <iostream>

#include <cstdlib>

#include <pthread.h>

#include <unistd.h>


using namespace std;


#define NUM_THREADS 5


void *wait(void *t) {
    int i;
    long tid;

    tid = (long)t;

    sleep(1);
    cout << "Sleeping in thread " << endl;
```

```cpp
      cout << "Thread with id : " << tid << "   ...exiting " << endl;
      pthread_exit(NULL);
}


int main () {
    int rc;
    int i;
    pthread_t threads[NUM_THREADS];
    pthread_attr_t attr;
    void *status;

    // Initialize and set thread joinable
    pthread_attr_init(&attr);
    pthread_attr_setdetachstate(&attr, PTHREAD_CREATE_JOINABLE);

    for( i = 0; i < NUM_THREADS; i++ ) {
       cout << "main() : creating thread, " << i << endl;
       rc = pthread_create(&threads[i], &attr, wait, (void *)i );
       if (rc) {
          cout << "Error:unable to create thread," << rc << endl;
          exit(-1);
       }
    }


    // free attribute and wait for the other threads
    pthread_attr_destroy(&attr);
    for( i = 0; i < NUM_THREADS; i++ ) {
       rc = pthread_join(threads[i], &status);
       if (rc) {
          cout << "Error:unable to join," << rc << endl;
          exit(-1);
       }
       cout << "Main: completed thread id :" << i ;
       cout << "  exiting with status :" << status << endl;
    }
```

```
    cout << "Main: program exiting." << endl;

    pthread_exit(NULL);

}
```

When the above code is compiled and executed, it produces the following result:

```
main() : creating thread, 0

main() : creating thread, 1

main() : creating thread, 2

main() : creating thread, 3

main() : creating thread, 4

Sleeping in thread

Thread with id : 0 .... exiting

Sleeping in thread

Thread with id : 1 .... exiting

Sleeping in thread

Thread with id : 2 .... exiting

Sleeping in thread

Thread with id : 3 .... exiting

Sleeping in thread

Thread with id : 4 .... exiting

Main: completed thread id :0  exiting with status :0

Main: completed thread id :1  exiting with status :0

Main: completed thread id :2  exiting with status :0

Main: completed thread id :3  exiting with status :0

Main: completed thread id :4  exiting with status :0

Main: program exiting.
```

Applications of C++

Games

C++ overrides the complexities of 3D games, optimizes resource management and facilitates multiplayer with networking. The language is extremely fast, allows procedural programming for CPU intensive functions and provides greater control over hardware, because of which it has been widely used in development of gaming engines. For instance, the science fiction game Doom 3 is cited as an example of a game that used C++ well and the Unreal Engine, a suite of game development tools, is written in C++.

Graphic User Interface based Applications

Many highly used applications, such as Image Ready, Adobe Premier, Photoshop and Illustrator, are scripted in C++.

Web Browsers

With the introduction of specialized languages such as PHP and Java, the adoption of C++ is limited for scripting of websites and web applications. However, where speed and reliability are required, C++ is still preferred. For instance, a part of Google's back-end is coded in C++, and the rendering engine of a few open source projects, such as web browser Mozilla Firefox and email client Mozilla Thunderbird, are also scripted in the programming language.

Advance Computations and Graphics

C++ provides the means for building applications requiring real-time physical simulations, high-performance image processing, and mobile sensor applications. Maya 3D software, used for integrated 3D modeling, visual effects and animation, is coded in C++.

Database Software

C++ and C have been used for scripting MySQL, one of the most popular database management software. The software forms the backbone of a variety of database-based enterprises.

Operating Systems

C++ forms an integral part of many of the prevalent operating systems including Apple's OS X and various versions of Microsoft Windows, and the erstwhile Symbian mobile OS.

Enterprise Software

C++ finds a purpose in banking and trading enterprise applications, such as those deployed by Bloomberg and Reuters. It is also used in development of advanced software, such as flight simulators and radar processing.

Medical and Engineering Applications

Many advanced medical equipments, such as MRI machines, use C++ language for scripting their software. It is also part of engineering applications, such as high-end CAD/CAM systems.

Compilers

A host of compilers including Apple C++, Bloodshed Dev-C++, Clang C++ and MINGW make use of C++ language. C and its successor C++ are leveraged for diverse software and platform development requirements, from operating systems to graphic designing applications. Further, these languages have assisted in the development of new languages for special purposes like C#, Java, PHP, Verilog etc.

References

- What-is-Cplusplus-programming-language: tutorialspoint.com, Retrieved 28 January, 2019

- Cpp-basic-syntax, core-tutorials: blog.miyozinc.com, Retrieved July 25, 2019

- C-data-types: geeksforgeeks.org, Retrieved 02 June, 2019

- Cpp-variable-types: tutorialspoint.com, Retrieved 28 July, 2019

- Decision-making-in-cpp: studytonight.com, Retrieved 26 June, 2019

- cpp-strings: w3schools.com, Retrieved 18 January, 2019

- Cpp-multithreading: tutorialspoint.com, Retrieved 15 May, 2019

- Applications-of-c-c-plus-plus-in-the-real-world: invensis.net, Retrieved 31 March, 2019

2
General Concepts of C++

C++ is a vast field of language comprising concepts of classes, auto-linking, Argument-Dependent Name Lookup, header file, one definition rule, run-time type information, sequence point, single compilation unit, undefined behavior, virtual function cells, etc. This chapter has been carefully written to provide an easy understanding of the varied concepts of C++.

Classes

The building block of C++ that leads to Object Oriented programming is a Class. It is a user defined data type, which holds its own data members and member functions, which can be accessed and used by creating an instance of that class. A class is like a blueprint for an object.

For Example: Consider the Class of Cars. There may be many cars with different names and brand but all of them will share some common properties like all of them will have 4 wheels, Speed Limit, Mileage range etc. So here, Car is the class and wheels, speed limits, mileage are their properties.

- A Class is a user defined data-type which has data members and member functions.

- Data members are the data variables and member functions are the functions used to manipulate these variables and together these data members and member functions defines the properties and behavior of the objects in a Class.

- In the above example of class Car, the data member will be speed limit, mileage etc and member functions can be apply brakes, increase speed etc.

An Object is an instance of a Class. When a class is defined, no memory is allocated but when it is instantiated (i.e. an object is created) memory is allocated.

Defining Class and Declaring Objects

A class is defined in C++ using keyword class followed by the name of class. The body of class is defined inside the curly brackets and terminated by a semicolon at the end.

Declaring Objects: When a class is defined, only the specification for the object is defined; no memory or storage is allocated. To use the data and access functions defined in the class, you need to create objects.

```
keyword        user-defined name


class ClassName

{  Access specifier:        //can be private,public or protected

   Data members;           // Variables to be used

   Member Functions() { }  //Methods to access data members

   };                      // Class name ends with a semicolon
```

Syntax

```
ClassName ObjectName;
```

Accessing data members and member functions: The data members and member functions of class can be accessed using the dot('.') operator with the object. For example if the name of object is obj and you want to access the member function with the name printName() then you will have to write obj.printName() .

Accessing Data Members

The public data members are also accessed in the same way given however the private data members are not allowed to be accessed directly by the object. Accessing a data member depends solely on the access control of that data member.

This access control is given by Access modifiers in C++. There are three access modifiers: `public`, `private` and `protected`.

```
// C++ program to demonstrate

// accessing of data members


#include <bits/stdc++.h>

using namespace std;

class Geeks

{

    // Access specifier

    public:


    // Data Members
```

```
    string geekname;


    // Member Functions()
    void printname()
    {
        cout << "Geekname is: " << geekname;

    }
};


int main() {


    // Declare an object of class geeks
    Geeks obj1;


    // accessing data member
    obj1.geekname = "Abhi";


    // accessing member function
    obj1.printname();
    return 0;

}
```

Output:

```
Geekname is: Abhi
```

Member Functions in Classes

There are 2 ways to define a member function:

- Inside class definition.

- Outside class definition.

To define a member function outside the class definition we have to use the scope resolution :: operator along with class name and function name.

```
// C++ program to demonstrate function

// declaration outside class
```

```cpp
#include <bits/stdc++.h>
using namespace std;
class Geeks
{
    public:
    string geekname;
    int id;

    // printname is not defined inside class definition
    void printname();

    // printid is defined inside class definition
    void printid()
    {
        cout << "Geek id is: " << id;
    }
};

// Definition of printname using scope resolution operator ::
void Geeks::printname()
{
    cout << "Geekname is: " << geekname;
}
int main() {

    Geeks obj1;
    obj1.geekname = "xyz";
    obj1.id=15;

    // call printname()
    obj1.printname();
```

```
    cout << endl;


    // call printid()

    obj1.printid();

    return 0;

}
```

Output:

```
Geekname is: xyz

Geek id is: 15
```

All the member functions defined inside the class definition are by default `inline`, but you can also make any non-class function inline by using keyword in line with them. Inline functions are actual functions, which are copied everywhere during compilation, like pre-processor macro, so the overhead of function calling is reduced.

Declaring a friend function is a way to give private access to a non-member function.

Constructors are special class members which are called by the compiler every time an object of that class is instantiated. Constructors have the same name as the class and may be defined inside or outside the class definition.

There are 3 types of constructors:

- Default constructors.

- Parametrized constructors.

- Copy constructors.

```
// C++ program to demonstrate constructors


#include <bits/stdc++.h>

using namespace std;

class Geeks

{

    public:

    int id;


    //Default Constructor

    Geeks()
```

```
    {
        cout << "Default Constructor called" << endl;
        id=-1;
    }


    //Parametrized Constructor
    Geeks(int x)
    {
        cout << "Parametrized Constructor called" << endl;
        id=x;
    }
};
int main() {

    // obj1 will call Default Constructor
    Geeks obj1;
    cout << "Geek id is: " <<obj1.id << endl;


    // obj1 will call Parametrized Constructor
    Geeks obj2(21);
    cout << "Geek id is: " <<obj2.id << endl;
    return 0;
}
```

Output:

```
Default Constructor called
Geek id is: -1
Parametrized Constructor called
Geek id is: 21
```

A `Copy Constructor` creates a new object, which is exact copy of the existing object. The compiler provides a default Copy Constructor to all the classes.

Syntax:

```
class-name (class-name &){}
```

Destructors

Destructor is another special member function that is called by the compiler when the scope of the object ends.

```cpp
// C++ program to explain destructors

#include <bits/stdc++.h>
using namespace std;
class Geeks
{
    public:
    int id;

    //Definition for Destructor
    ~Geeks()
    {
        cout << «Destructor called for id: « << id <<endl;
    }
};

int main()
{
    Geeks obj1;
    obj1.id=7;
    int i = 0;
    while ( i < 5 )
    {
        Geeks obj2;
        obj2.id=i;
        i++;
    } // Scope for obj2 ends here

    return 0;
} // Scope for obj1 ends here
```

Output:

```
Destructor called for id: 0
```

```
Destructor called for id: 1
Destructor called for id: 2
Destructor called for id: 3
Destructor called for id: 4
Destructor called for id: 7
```

Auto-linking

Auto-linking is a mechanism for automatically determining which libraries to link to while building a C, C++ or Obj-C program. It is activated by means of `#pragma comment(lib, <name>)` statements in the header files of the library, or `@import <name>` depending on the compiler.

Most Windows compilers support auto-linking, as does Clang, while GCC does not support auto-linking.

Argument-dependent Name Lookup

In the C++ programming language, argument-dependent lookup (ADL), or argument-dependent name lookup, applies to the lookup of an unqualified function name depending on the types of the arguments given to the function call. This behavior is also known as Koenig lookup, as it is often attributed to Andrew Koenig, though he is not its inventor.

During argument-dependent lookup, other namespaces not considered during normal lookup may be searched where the set of namespaces to be searched depends on the types of the function arguments. Specifically, the set of declarations discovered during the ADL process, and considered for resolution of the function name, is the union of the declarations found by normal lookup with the declarations found by looking in the set of namespaces associated with the types of the function arguments.

Example:

An example of ADL looks like this:

```
namespace NS {

class A {};

void f(A& a, int i) {}

}  // namespace NS

int main() {
```

```
    NS::A a;

    f(a, 0);   // Calls NS::f.

}
```

Even though the `main` function is not in namespace NS, nor is namespace NS in scope, the function `NS:f(A&, int)` is found because of the declared types of the actual parameters in the function call statement.

A common pattern in the C++ Standard Library is to declare overloaded operators that will be found in this manner. For example, this simple Hello World program would not compile if it weren't for ADL:

```
#include <iostream>

#include <string>


int main() {

  std::string str = "hello world";

  std::cout << str;

}
```

Using `<<` is equivalent to calling `operator<<` without the `std::` qualifier. However, in this case, the overload of `operator<<` that works for `string` is in the `std` namespace, so ADL is required for it to be used.

The following code would work without ADL (which is applied to it anyway):

```
#include <iostream>


int main() {

  std::cout << 5;

}
```

It works because the output operator for integers is a member function of the `std::ostream` class, which is the type of `cout`. Thus, the compiler interprets this statement as:

```
std::cout.operator<<(5);
```

which it can resolve during normal lookup. However, consider that e.g. the `const char *` overloaded `operator<<` is a non-member function in the `std` namespace and, thus, requires ADL for a correct lookup:

```
/* will print the provided char string as expected using ADL derived from the argument
type std::cout */

operator<<(std::cout, "Hi there")
```

```
/* calls a ostream member function of the operator<< taking a void const*,
```

which will print the address of the provided char string instead of the content of the char string */

```
std::cout.operator<<("Hi there")
```

The std namespace overloaded non-member operator<< function to handle strings is another example:

```
/*equivalent to operator<<(std::cout, str). The compiler searches the std namespace using
ADL due to the type std::string of the str parameter and std::cout */
```

```
std::cout << str;
```

As Koenig points out in a personal note,without ADL the compiler would indicate an error stating it could not find operator<< as the statement doesn't explicitly specify that it is found in the std namespace.

Interfaces

Functions found by ADL are considered part of a class's interface. In the C++ Standard Library, several algorithms use unqualified calls to swap from within the std namespace. As a result, the generic std::swap function is used if nothing else is found, but if these algorithms are used with a third-party class, Foo, found in another namespace that also contains swap(Foo&, Foo&), that overload of swap will be used.

Header File

Header files contain definitions of Functions and Variables, which is imported or used into any C++ program by using the pre-processor #include statement. Header file have an extension ".h" which contains C++ function declaration and macro definition.

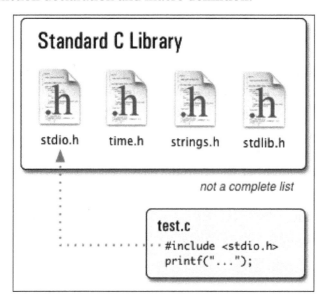

Each header file contains information (or declarations) for a particular group of functions. Like `stdio.h` header file contains declarations of standard input and output functions available in C++ which is used for get the input and print the output. Similarly, the header file `math.h` contains declarations of mathematical functions available in C++.

Types of Header Files in C++

- System header files: It is comes with compiler.
- User header files: It is written by programmer.

The Need for Header File

When we want to use any function in our C++ program then first we need to import their definition from C++ library, for importing their declaration and definition we need to include header file in program by using #include. Header file include at the top of any C++ program.

For example if we use clrscr() in C++ program, then we need to include, conio.h header file, because in conio.h header file definition of clrscr() (for clear screen) is written in conio.h header file.

Syntax:

```
#include<conio.h>
```

Syntax:

```
#include<iostream>


int main()
{
    using namespace std;
    cout << "Hello, world!" << endl;
    return 0;
}
```

In above program print message on scree hello world! by using cout but we don't define cout here actually already cout has been declared in a header file called `iostream`.

Using Header File in a Program

Both user and system header files are include using the pre-processing directive #include. It has following two forms:

Syntax:

```
#include<file>
```

This form is used for system header files. It searches for a file named file in a standard list of system directives.

Syntax:

```
#include"file"
```

This form used for header files of our own program. It searches for a file named file in the directive containing the current file.

One Definition Rule

The One Definition Rule (ODR) is an important concept in the C++ programming language. It is defined in the ISO C++ Standard (ISO/IEC 14882) 2003.

In short, the ODR states that:

- In any translation unit, a template, type, function, or object can have no more than one definition. Some of these can have any number of declarations. A definition provides an instance.

- In the entire program, an object or non-inline function cannot have more than one definition; if an object or function is used, it must have exactly one definition. You can declare an object or function that is never used, in which case you don't have to provide a definition. In no event can there be more than one definition.

- Some things, like types, templates, and extern inline functions, can be defined in more than one translation unit. For a given entity, each definition must have the same sequence of tokens. Non-extern objects and functions in different translation units are different entities, even if their names and types are the same.

Some violations of the ODR must be diagnosed by the compiler. Other violations, particularly those that span translation units, are not required to be diagnosed.

Examples:

In general, a translation unit shall contain no more than one definition of any class type. In this example, two definitions of the class type C occur in the same translation unit. This typically occurs if a header file is included twice by the same source file without appropriate header guards.

```
class C {}; // first definition of C

class C {}; // error, second definition of C
```

In the following, forming a pointer to S or defining a function taking a reference to S are examples of legal constructs, because they do not require the type of S to be complete. Therefore, a definition is not required.

Defining an object of type S, a function taking an argument of type S, or using S in a sizeof expression are examples of contexts where S must be complete, and therefore require a definition.

```
struct S;      // declaration of S

S * p;         // ok, no definition required

void f(S&);    // ok, no definition required

void f(S*);    // ok, no definition required

S f();         // ok, no definition required - this is a function declaration only!


S s;           // error, definition required

sizeof(S);     // error, definition required
```

In certain cases, there can be more than one definition of a type or a template. A program consisting of multiple header files and source files will typically have more than one definition of a type, but not more than one definition per translation unit.

If a program contains more than one definition of a type, then each definition must be equivalent.

Static Const Data Members

In pre-standard C++, all static data members required a definition outside of their class. However, during the C++ standardization process it was decided to lift this requirement for static const integral members. The intent was to allow uses such as:

```
struct C {

  static const int N = 10;

};

char data[C::N]; // N "used" without out-of-class definition
```

without a namespace scope definition for N.

Nevertheless, the wording of the 1998 C++ standard still required a definition if the member was used in the program. This included the member appearing anywhere except as the operand to sizeof or typeid, effectively making the above ill-formed.

This was identified as a defect, and the wording was adjusted to allow such a member to appear anywhere a constant expression is required, without requiring an out-of-class definition. This includes array bounds, case expressions, static member initializers, and nontype template arguments.

```
struct C {

  static const int N = 10;

  static const int U = N; // Legal per C++03
```

```
};
```

```
char data[C::N]; // Legal per C++03
```

```
template<int> struct D;
```

```
template<> struct D<C::N> {}; // Legal per C++03
```

However, using a static const integral member anywhere except where an integral constant-expression is required, requires a definition:

```
struct C {
  static const int N = 10;
};
```

```
int main() {
  int i = C::N; // Ill-formed. Definition of C::N required.
}
```

This requirement was relaxed in a later standard, C++11.

Example Showing Unexpected Side Effects

We need 4 files: "odr.h", "main.cpp", "odr1.cpp", "odr2.cpp"

The acronym "odr" here is short for "One Definition Rule".

odr.h:

```
/// abstract base class
class CBase {
public:
        virtual void xxx() = 0;
        virtual ~CBase() = default;
};
```

```
extern CBase *odr1_create();
extern CBase *odr2_create();
```

main.cpp

```
#include "odr.h"


int main(int argc, char **argv)

{

        CBase *o1 = odr1_create();

        CBase *o2 = odr2_create();

        o1->xxx();

        o2->xxx();

}
```

odr1.cpp

```
#include <stdio.h>

#include "odr.h"


class CDummy : public CBase {

public:

        void xxx() override {

                printf("odr ONE dummy: Hello\n");

        }

};


CBase *odr1_create() {

        return new CDummy();

}
```

odr2.cpp

```
#include <stdio.h>

#include "odr.h"


class CDummy : public CBase {

public:

        void xxx() override {

                printf("odr TWO dummy: World\n");

        }
```

```
};


CBase *odr2_create() {

        return new CDummy();

}
```

Under a Linux shell to try out, compile with:

```
g++ -c odr1.cpp
```

```
g++ -c odr2.cpp
```

```
g++ -c main.cpp
```

```
g++ -o odr main.o odr1.o odr2.o
```

Under a Windows Visual Studio "Build Tools Command Prompt", compile with:

```
cl /c main.cpp
```

```
cl /c odr1.cpp
```

```
cl /c odr2.cpp
```

```
cl /Feodr.exe main.obj odr1.obj odr2.obj
```

When executed the expected output is:

```
odr ONE dummy: Hello
```

```
odr TWO dummy: World
```

But you very likely get:

```
odr ONE dummy: Hello
```

```
odr ONE dummy: Hello
```

The problem is, that the C++ linker has to figure out how to build the virtual method table for the (two different) "CDummy" classes, and that only works if the class names are different.

Run-time Type Information

In computer programming, run-time type information or run-time type identification (RTTI) is a feature of the C++ programming language that exposes information about an object's data type at runtime. Run-time type information can apply to simple data types, such as integers and characters, or to generic types. This is a C++ specialization of a more general concept called type introspection. Similar mechanisms are also known in other programming languages, such as Object Pascal (Delphi).

In the original C++ design, Bjarne Stroustrup did not include run-time type information, because he thought this mechanism was often misused.

C++ RTTI can be used to do safe typecasts, using the `dynamic_cast<>` operator, and to manipulate type information at run time, using the `typeid` operator and `std::type_info` class.

RTTI is available only for classes that are polymorphic, which means they have at least one virtual method. In practice, this is not a limitation because base classes must have a virtual destructor to allow objects of derived classes to perform proper cleanup if they are deleted from a base pointer.

RTTI is optional with some compilers; the programmer can choose at compile time whether to include the functionality. There may be a resource cost to making RTTI available even if a program does not use it.

Typeid

The `typeid` keyword is used to determine the class of an object at run time. It returns a reference to `std::type_info` object, which exists until the end of the program. The use of `typeid`, in a non-polymorphic context, is often preferred over `dynamic_cast<class_type>` in situations where just the class information is needed, because `typeid` is always a constant-time procedure, whereas `dynamic_cast` may need to traverse the class derivation lattice of its argument at runtime. Some aspects of the returned object are implementation-defined, such as `std::type_info::name()`, and cannot be relied on across compilers to be consistent.

Objects of class `std::bad_typeid` are thrown when the expression for `typeid` is the result of applying the unary * operator on a null pointer. Whether an exception is thrown for other null reference arguments is implementation-dependent. In other words, for the exception to be guaranteed, the expression must take the form `typeid(*p)` where `p` is any expression resulting in a null pointer.

Example:

```
#include <iostream>

#include <typeinfo>


class Person {

public:

    virtual ~Person() = default;

};


class Employee : public Person {};


int main() {

    Person person;

    Employee employee;
```

```
Person* ptr = &employee;

Person& ref = employee;


// The string returned by typeid::name is implementation-defined.
std::cout << typeid(person).name()

        << std::endl;  // Person (statically known at compile-time).
std::cout << typeid(employee).name()

        << std::endl;  // Employee (statically known at compile-time).
std::cout << typeid(ptr).name()

        << std::endl;  // Person* (statically known at compile-time).
std::cout << typeid(*ptr).name()

        << std::endl;  // Employee (looked up dynamically at run-time

                       //           because it is the dereference of a

                       //           pointer to a polymorphic class).
std::cout << typeid(ref).name()

        << std::endl;  // Employee (references can also be polymorphic)


Person* p = nullptr;


try {

    typeid(*p); // Not undefined behavior; throws std::bad_typeid.
} catch (...) { }


Person& p_ref = *p; // Undefined behavior: dereferencing null
typeid(p_ref);       // does not meet requirements to throw std::bad_typeid

                     // because the expression for typeid is not the result

                     // of applying the unary * operator.
}
```

Output (exact output varies by system and compiler):

```
Person

Employee

Person*
```

```
Employee

Employee
```

Dynamic_cast and Java Cast

The `dynamic_cast` operator in C++ is used for downcasting a reference or pointer to a more specific type in the class hierarchy. Unlike the `static_cast`, the target of the `dynamic_cast` must be a pointer or reference to class. Unlike `static_cast` and C-style typecast (where type check is made during compilation), a type safety check is performed at runtime. If the types are not compatible, an exception will be thrown (when dealing with references) or a null pointer will be returned (when dealing with pointers).

A Java typecast behaves similarly; if the object being cast is not actually an instance of the target type, and cannot be converted to one by a language-defined method, an instance of `java.lang.ClassCastException` will be thrown.

Example:

Suppose some function takes an object of type `A` as its argument, and wishes to perform some additional operation if the object passed is an instance of `B`, a subclass of `A`. This can be accomplished using `dynamic_cast` as follows.

```cpp
#include <array>

#include <iostream>

#include <memory>

#include <typeinfo>


using namespace std;


class A {

public:

    // Since RTTI is included in the virtual method table there should be at

    // least one virtual function.

    virtual ~A() = default;


    void MethodSpecificToA() {

        cout << "Method specific for A was invoked" << endl;

    }

};
```

```cpp
class B: public A {
public:

    void MethodSpecificToB() {

        cout << "Method specific for B was invoked" << endl;

    }

};


void MyFunction(A& my_a) {

    try {

        // Cast will be successful only for B type objects.

        B& my_b = dynamic_cast<B&>(my_a);

        my_b.MethodSpecificToB();

    } catch (const bad_cast& e) {

        cerr << " Exception " << e.what() << " thrown." << endl;

        cerr << " Object is not of type B" << endl;

    }

}


int main() {

    array<unique_ptr<A>, 3> array_of_a; // Array of pointers to base class A.

    array_of_a[0] = make_unique<B>();   // Pointer to B object.

    array_of_a[1] = make_unique<B>();   // Pointer to B object.

    array_of_a[2] = make_unique<A>();   // Pointer to A object.


    for (int i = 0; i < 3; ++i)

        MyFunction(*array_of_a[i]);

}
```

Console output:

```
Method specific for B was invoked
Method specific for B was invoked
Exception std::bad_cast thrown.
Object is not of type B
```

A similar version of `MyFunction` can be written with pointers instead of references:

```
void MyFunction(A* my_a) {

    B* my_b = dynamic_cast<B*>(my_a);


    if (my_b != nullptr)

        my_b->methodSpecificToB();

    else

        std::cerr << "  Object is not B type" << std::endl;

}
```

Sequence Point

A sequence point defines any point in a computer program's execution at which it is guaranteed that all side effects of previous evaluations will have been performed, and no side effects from subsequent evaluations have yet been performed. They are often mentioned in reference to C and C++, because they are a core concept for determining the validity and, if valid, the possible results of expressions. Adding more sequence points is sometimes necessary to make an expression defined and to ensure a single valid order of evaluation.

With C++11, usage of the term sequence point has been replaced by sequencing. There are three possibilities:

- An expression's evaluation can be sequenced before that of another expression, or equivalently the other expression's evaluation is sequenced after that of the first.

- The expressions' evaluation is indeterminately sequenced, meaning one is sequenced before the other, but which is unspecified.

- The expressions' evaluation is unsequenced.

The execution of unsequenced evaluations can overlap, with catastrophic undefined behavior if they share state. This situation can arise in parallel computations, causing race conditions. However, it can already arise in simple non-concurrent situations like `(a = 1) + (b = a)`, where part of the assignment to `a` (eg., half of the bits) may happen before `b = a`, and the rest afterwards, such that after evaluation of the expression, `b` may contain a meaningless intermediate state of `a`.

Examples of Ambiguity

Consider two functions `f()` and `g()`. In C and C++, the + operator is not associated with a sequence point, and therefore in the expression `f()+g()` it is possible that either `f()` or `g()` will be executed first. The comma operator introduces a sequence point, and therefore in the code `f(),g()` the order of evaluation is defined: first `f()` is called, and then `g()` is called.

Sequence points also come into play when the same variable is modified more than once within a single expression. An often-cited example is the C expression `i=i++`, which apparently both assigns `i` its previous value and increments `i`. The final value of `i` is ambiguous, because, depending on the order of expression evaluation, the increment may occur before, after, or interleaved with the assignment. The definition of a particular language might specify one of the possible behaviors or simply say the behavior is undefined. In C and C++, evaluating such an expression yields undefined behavior. Other languages, such as C#, define the precedence of the assignment and increment operator in such a way that the result of the expression `i=i++` is guaranteed.

Sequence Points in C and C++

In C and C++, sequence points occur in the following places. (In C++, overloaded operators act like functions, and thus operators that have been overloaded introduce sequence points in the same way as function calls).

- Between evaluation of the left and right operands of the && (logical AND), || (logical OR) (as part of short-circuit evaluation), and comma operators. For example, in the expression `*p++ != 0 && *q++ != 0`, all side effects of the sub-expression `*p++ != 0` are completed before any attempt to access `q`.

- Between the evaluation of the first operand of the ternary "question-mark" operator and the second or third operand. For example, in the expression `a = (*p++) ? (*p++) : 0` there is a sequence point after the first `*p++`, meaning it has already been incremented by the time the second instance is executed.

- At the end of a full expression. This category includes expression statements (such as the assignment `a=b;`), return statements, the controlling expressions of if, switch, while, or do-while statements, and all three expressions in a for statement.

- Before a function is entered in a function call. The order in which the arguments are evaluated is not specified, but this sequence point means that all of their side effects are complete before the function is entered. In the expression `f(i++) + g(j++) + h(k++)`, f is called with a parameter of the original value of `i`, but `i` is incremented before entering the body of `f`. Similarly, `j` and k are updated before entering g and h respectively. However, it is not specified in which order `f()`, `g()`, `h()` are executed, nor in which order `i`, `j`, k are incremented. If the body of f accesses the variables `j` and `k`, it might find both, neither, or just one of them to have been incremented. (The function call `f(a,b,c)` is *not* a use of the comma operator; the order of evaluation for `a`, `b`, and `c` is unspecified).

- At a function return, after the return value is copied into the calling context. (This sequence point is only specified in the C++ standard; it is present only implicitly in C.)

- At the end of an initializer; for example, after the evaluation of 5 in the declaration `int a = 5;`.

- Between each declarator in each declarator sequence; for example, between the two evaluations of `a++` in `int x = a++, y = a++`. (This is *not* an example of the comma operator).

- After each conversion associated with an input/output format specifier. For example, in the expression `printf "foo %n %d", &a, 42)`, there is a sequence point after the `%n` is evaluated and before printing 42.

Single Compilation Unit

Single Compilation Unit (SCU) is a computer programming technique for the C and C++ languages, which reduces compilation time for programs spanning multiple files. Specifically, it allows the compiler to keep data from shared header files, definitions and templates, so that it need not recreate them for each file. It is an instance of program optimization. The technique can be applied to an entire program or to some subset of source files; when applied to an entire program, it is also known as a unity build.

Purpose

In the C/C++ compilation model (formally "translation environment"), individual `.c`/`.cpp` source files are preprocessed into translation units, which are then translated (compiled) separately by the compiler into multiple object (`.o or .obj`) files. These object files can then be linked together to create a single executable file or library. However, this leads to multiple passes being performed on common header files, and with C++, multiple template instantiations of the same templates in different translation units.

The Single Compilation Unit technique uses pre-processor directives to "glue" different translation units together at compile time rather than at link time. This reduces the overall build time, due to eliminating the duplication, but increases the incremental build time (the time required after making a change to any single source file that is included in the Single Compilation Unit), due to requiring a full rebuild of the entire unit if any single input file changes. Therefore, this technique is appropriate for a set of infrequently modified source files with significant overlap (many or expensive common headers or templates), or source files that frequently require recompilation together, such as due to all including a common header or template that changes frequently.

Another disadvantage of SCU is that it is serial, compiling all included source files in sequence in one process, and thus cannot be parallelized, as can be done in separate compilation (via distcc or similar programs). Thus SCU requires explicit partitioning (manual partitioning or "sharding" into multiple units) to parallelize compilation.

SCU also allows an optimizing compiler to perform interprocedural optimization without requiring link-time optimization, therefore allowing optimizations such as inlining, and helps avoiding implicit code bloat due to exceptions, side effects, and register allocation. These optimizations are often not possible in many compilers, due to independent compilation, where optimization happens separately in each translation unit during *compilation,* but the "dumb linker" simply links object files, without performing any optimizations itself, and thus interprocedural optimization between translation units is not possible.

Example:

For example, if you have the source files foo.cpp and bar.cpp, they can be placed in a Single Compilation Unit as follows:

```
#include "foo.cpp"

#include "bar.cpp"
```

Suppose foo.cpp and bar.cpp are:

```
//foo.cpp

#include <iostream> // A large, standard header

#include "bar.h"    // Declaration of function 'bar'


int main()          // Definition of function 'main'
{

  bar();

}
//bar.cpp

#include <iostream> // The same large, standard header


void bar()          // Definition of function 'bar'
{

  ...

}
```

Now the standard header file (iostream) is compiled only once, and function bar may be inlined into function main, despite being from another module.

Undefined Behavior

In computer programming, undefined behavior (UB) is the result of executing computer code whose behavior is not prescribed by the language specification to which the code adheres, for the current state of the program. This happens when the translator of the source code makes certain assumptions, but these assumptions are not satisfied during execution.

The behavior of some programming languages—most famously C and C++—is undefined in some cases. In the standards for these languages the semantics of certain operations is described as *undefined*. These cases typically represent unambiguous bugs in the code, for example indexing an array outside of its bounds. An implementation is allowed to assume that such operations never occur in correct standard-conforming program code. In the case of C/C++, the compiler is allowed to give a compile-time diagnostic in these cases, but is not required to: the implementation will be considered correct whatever it does in such cases, analogous to don't-care terms in digital logic. It is the responsibility of the programmer to write code that never invokes undefined behavior, although compiler implementations are allowed to issue diagnostics when this happens. This assumption can make various program transformations valid or simplify their proof of correctness, giving flexibility to the implementation. As a result, the compiler can often make more optimizations. It also allows more compile-time checks by both compilers and static program analysis.

In the C community, undefined behavior may be humorously referred to as "nasal demons", after a comp.std.c post that explained undefined behavior as allowing the compiler to do anything it chooses, even "to make demons fly out of your nose". Under some circumstances there can be specific restrictions on undefined behavior. For example, the instruction set specifications of a CPU might leave the behavior of some forms of an instruction undefined, but if the CPU supports memory protection then the specification will probably include a blanket rule stating that no user-accessible instruction may cause a hole in the operating system's security; so an actual CPU would be permitted to corrupt user registers in response to such an instruction, but would not be allowed to, for example, switch into supervisor mode.

Benefits

Documenting an operation as undefined behavior allows compilers to assume that this operation will never happen in a conforming program. This gives the compiler more information about the code and this information can lead to more optimization opportunities.

An example for the C language:

```
int foo(unsigned char x)

{

    int value = 2147483600; /* assuming 32 bit int */

    value += x;

    if (value < 2147483600)

        bar();

    return value;

}
```

The value of x cannot be negative and, given that signed integer overflow is undefined behavior in C, the compiler can assume that value < 2147483600 will always be false. Thus the if statement, including the call to the function bar, can be ignored by the compiler since the test expression in the if has no side effects and its condition will never be satisfied. The code is therefore semantically equivalent to:

```
int foo(unsigned char x)

{

    int value = 2147483600;

    value += x;

    return value;

}
```

Had the compiler been forced to assume that signed integer overflow has *wraparound* behavior, then the transformation above would not have been legal.

Such optimizations become hard to spot by humans when the code is more complex and other optimizations, like inlining, take place. For example, another function may call the above function:

```
void run_tasks(unsigned char *ptrx) {

    int z;

    z = foo(*ptrx);

    while (*ptrx > 60) {

        run_one_task(ptrx, z);

    }

}
```

The compiler is free to optimize away the `while`-loop here by applying value range analysis: by inspecting `foo()`, it knows that the initial value pointed to by `ptrx` cannot possibly exceed 47 (as any more would trigger undefined behavior in `foo()`), therefore the initial check of `*ptrx > 60` will always be false in a conforming program. Going further, since the result z is now never used and `foo()` has no side-effects, the compiler can optimize `run_tasks()` to be an empty function that returns immediately. The disappearance of the while-loop may be especially surprising if `foo()` is defined in a separately compiled object file.

Another benefit from allowing signed integer overflow to be undefined is that it makes it possible to store and manipulate a variable's value in a processor register that is larger than the size of the variable in the source code. For example, if the type of a variable as specified in the source code is narrower than the native register width (such as "int" on a 64-bit machine, a common scenario), then the compiler can safely use a signed 64-bit integer for the variable in the machine code it produces, without changing the defined behavior of the code. If a program depended on the behavior of a 32-bit integer overflow, then a compiler would have to insert additional logic when compiling for a 64-bit machine, because the overflow behavior of most machine instructions depends on the register width.

A further important benefit of undefined signed integer overflow is that it enables, though does not require, erroneous overflows to be detected at compile-time or by static program analysis, or by run-time checks such as the Clang and GCC sanitizers and valgrind; if such overflow were defined with semantics such as wrap-around then compile-time checks would not be possible.

Risks

C and C++ standards have several forms of undefined behavior throughout, which offer increased liberty in compiler implementations and compile-time checks at the expense of undefined run-time behavior if present. In particular, the ISO C standard has an appendix listing common sources of undefined behavior. Moreover, compilers are not required to diagnose code that relies on undefined behavior. Hence, it is common for programmers, even experienced ones, to rely on undefined behavior either by mistake, or simply because they are not well-versed in the rules of the language that can span hundreds of pages. This can result in bugs that are exposed when a different compiler, or different settings, are used. Testing or fuzzing with dynamic undefined behavior checks enabled, e.g. the Clang sanitizers, can help to catch undefined behavior not diagnosed by the compiler or static analyzers.

In scenarios where security is critical, undefined behavior can lead to security vulnerabilities in software. When GCC's developers changed their compiler in 2008 such that it omitted certain overflow checks that relied on undefined behavior, CERT issued a warning against the newer versions of the compiler. Linux Weekly News pointed out that the same behavior was observed in PathScale C, Microsoft Visual C++ 2005 and several other compilers; the warning was later amended to warn about various compilers.

Examples in C and C++

The major forms of undefined behavior in C can be broadly classified as : spatial memory safety violations, temporal memory safety violations, integer overflow, strict aliasing violations, alignment violations, unsequenced modifications, data races, and loops that neither perform I/O nor terminate.

In C the use of any automatic variable before it has been initialized yields undefined behavior, as does integer division by zero, signed integer overflow, indexing an array outside of its defined bounds or null pointer dereferencing. In general, any instance of undefined behavior leaves the abstract execution machine in an unknown state, and causes the behavior of the entire program to be undefined.

Attempting to modify a string literal causes undefined behavior:

```
char *p = "wikipedia"; // valid C, deprecated in C++98/C++03, ill-formed as of C++11

p[0] = 'W'; // undefined behavior
```

Integer division by zero results in undefined behavior:

```
int x = 1;

return x / 0; // undefined behavior
```

Certain pointer operations may result in undefined behavior:

```
int arr[4] = {0, 1, 2, 3};

int *p = arr + 5;   // undefined behavior for indexing out of bounds

p = 0;

int a = *p;         // undefined behavior for dereferencing a null pointer
```

In C and C++, the comparison of pointers to objects is only strictly defined if the pointers point to members of the same object, or elements of the same array.

Example:

```
int main(void)

{

  int a = 0;
```

```
    int b = 0;

    return &a < &b; /* undefined behavior */
}
```

Reaching the end of a value-returning function (other than main()) without a return statement results in undefined behavior if the value of the function call is used by the caller:

```
int f()

{

}   /* undefined behavior if the value of the function call is used*/
```

Modifying an object between two sequence points more than once produces undefined behavior. There are considerable changes in what causes undefined behavior in relation to sequence points as of C++11. The following example will however cause undefined behavior in both C++ and C.

```
i = i++ + 1; // undefined behavior
```

When modifying an object between two sequence points, reading the value of the object for any other purpose than determining the value to be stored is also undefined behavior.

```
a[i] = i++; // undefined behavior

printf("%d %d\n", ++n, power(2, n)); // also undefined behavior
```

In C/C++ bitwise shifting a value by a number of bits which is either a negative number or is greater than or equal to the total number of bits in this value results in undefined behavior. The safest way (regardless a compiler vendor) is to always keep the number of bits to shift (the right operand of the << and >> bitwise operators) within the range: <0, sizeof(value)*CHAR_BIT - 1> (where value is the left operand).

```
int num = -1;

unsigned int val = 1 << num; //shifting by a negative number - undefined behavior


num = 32; //or whatever number greater than 31

val = 1 << num; //the literal '1' is typed as a 32-bit integer - in this case shifting
by more than 31 bits is undefined behavior


num = 64; //or whatever number greater than 63

unsigned long long val2 = 1ULL << num; //the literal '1ULL' is typed as a 64-bit integer
- in this case shifting by more than 63 bits is undefined behavior
```

Virtual Function Calls

A virtual function a member function which is declared within a base class and is redefined (Overriden) by a derived class. When you refer to a derived class object using a pointer or a reference to the base class, you can call a virtual function for that object and execute the derived class's version of the function.

- Virtual functions ensure that the correct function is called for an object, regardless of the type of reference (or pointer) used for function call.

- They are mainly used to achieve Runtime polymorphism

- Functions are declared with a virtual keyword in base class.

- The resolving of function call is done at Run-time.

Rules for Virtual Functions

- Virtual functions cannot be static and also cannot be a friend function of another class.

- Virtual functions should be accessed using pointer or reference of base class type to achieve run time polymorphism.

- The prototype of virtual functions should be same in base as well as derived class.

- They are always defined in base class and overridden in derived class. It is not mandatory for derived class to override (or re-define the virtual function), in that case base class version of function is used.

- A class may have virtual destructor but it cannot have a virtual constructor.

Compile-time vs. Run-time Behavior of Virtual Functions

Consider the following simple program showing run-time behavior of virtual functions.

```cpp
// CPP program to illustrate
// concept of Virtual Functions

#include <iostream>
using namespace std;

class base {
public:
    virtual void print()
    {
        cout << "print base class" << endl;
    }

    void show()
    {
```

```cpp
        cout << "show base class" << endl;
    }
};


class derived : public base {
public:
    void print()
    {
        cout << "print derived class" << endl;
    }

    void show()
    {
        cout << "show derived class" << endl;
    }
};


int main()
{
    base* bptr;
    derived d;
    bptr = &d;

    // virtual function, binded at runtime
    bptr->print();

    // Non-virtual function, binded at compile time
    bptr->show();
}
```

Output:

```
print derived class

show base class
```

Runtime polymorphism is achieved only through a pointer (or reference) of base class type. Also, a base class pointer can point to the objects of base class as well as to the objects of derived class. In above code, base class pointer 'bptr' contains the address of object 'd' of derived class.

Late binding(Runtime) is done in accordance with the content of pointer (i.e. location pointed to by pointer) and Early binding(Compile time) is done according to the type of pointer, since print() function is declared with virtual keyword so it will be bound at run-time (output is print derived class as pointer is pointing to object of derived class) and show() is non-virtual so it will be bound during compile time(output is show base class as pointer is of base type).

If we have created a virtual function in the base class and it is being overridden in the derived class then we don't need virtual keyword in the derived class, functions are automatically considered as virtual functions in the derived class.

Working of Virtual Functions

If a class contains a virtual function then compiler itself does two things:

- If object of that class is created then a virtual pointer(VPTR) is inserted as a data member of the class to point to VTABLE of that class. For each new object created, a new virtual pointer is inserted as a data member of that class.

- Irrespective of object is created or not, a static array of function pointer called VTABLE where each cell contains the address of each virtual function contained in that class.

Consider the example below:

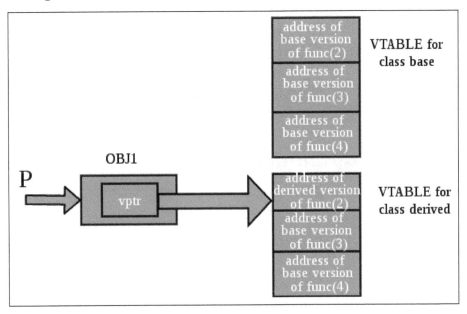

```
// CPP program to illustrate

// working of Virtual Functions

#include <iostream>

using namespace std;


class base {
```

```cpp
public:
    void fun_1() { cout << "base-1\n"; }
    virtual void fun_2() { cout << "base-2\n"; }
    virtual void fun_3() { cout << "base-3\n"; }
    virtual void fun_4() { cout << "base-4\n"; }
};


class derived : public base {
public:
    void fun_1() { cout << "derived-1\n"; }
    void fun_2() { cout << "derived-2\n"; }
    void fun_4(int x) { cout << "derived-4\n"; }
};


int main()
{
    base* p;
    derived obj1;
    p = &obj1;

    // Early binding because fun1() is non-virtual
    // in base
    p->fun_1();

    // Late binding (RTP)
    p->fun_2();

    // Late binding (RTP)
    p->fun_3();

    // Late binding (RTP)
    p->fun_4();
```

```
    // Early binding but this function call is

    // illegal(produces error) becasue pointer

    // is of base type and function is of

    // derived class

    // p->fun_4(5);

}
```

Output:

```
base-1

derived-2

base-3

base-4
```

Initially, we create a pointer of type base class and initialize it with the address of the derived class object. When we create an object of the derived class, the compiler creates a pointer as a data member of the class containing the address of VTABLE of the derived class.

Similar concept of Late and Early Binding is used as in above example. For fun_1() function call, base class version of function is called, fun_2() is overridden in derived class so derived class version is called, fun_3() is not overridden in derived class and is virtual function so base class version is called, similarly fun_4() is not overridden so base class version is called.

fun_4(int) in derived class is different from virtual function fun_4() in base class as prototype of both the function is different.

References

- C-classes-and-objects: geeksforgeeks.org, Retrieved 23 April, 2019
- Cpp-header-files: sitesbay.com, Retrieved 19 August, 2019
- Virtual-function-cpp: geeksforgeeks.org, Retrieved 28 April, 2019
- Peter van der Linden, Expert C Programming. ISBN 0-13-177429-8

3

C++ Language Extension

An extension is a programming language interpreter provided by an application program, used by the user to write macros or even a whole program. Cilk Plus, AspectC++, C++/CLI, C++/CX, CUDA C/C++, etc. are some of the C++ extensions that fall under this domain. This chapter discusses in detail these C++ language extensions.

Cilk Plus

Intel Cilk Plus is an extension to the C and C++ languages to support data and task parallelism which is being deprecated in the 2018 release of Intel Software Development Tools. It will remain in deprecation mode in the Intel C++ Compiler for an extended period of two years. Intel Cilk Plus adds simple language extensions to the C and C++ languages to express task and data parallelism. These language extensions are powerful, yet easy to apply and use in a wide range of applications.

Intel Cilk Plus includes the following features and benefits:

Feature	Benefit
Keywords	Simple, powerful expression of task parallelism: • `cilk_for` - Parallelize for loops. • `cilk_spawn` - Specifies that a function can execute in parallel with the remainder of the calling function. • `cilk_sync` - Specifies that all spawned calls in a function must complete before execution continues.
Reducers	Eliminate contention for shared variables among tasks by automatically creating views of them as needed and "reducing" them in a lock free manner.
Array Notation	Data parallelism for arrays or sections of arrays.
SIMD-Enabled Functions	Define functions that can be vectorized when called from within an array notation expression or a #pragma simd loop.
#pragma simd	Specifies that a loop is to be vectorized.

Serial Semantics

A deterministic Intel Cilk Plus application has serial semantics. That is, the result of a parallel run is the same as if the program had executed serially. Serial semantics makes it easier to reason about the parallel application. In addition, developers can use familiar tools to debug the application.

Cilk Keywords

Intel Cilk Plus adds three keywords to C and C++ to allow developers to express opportunities for parallelism.

- `Cilk_spawn`: Specifies that a function call can execute asynchronously, without requiring the caller to wait for it to return. This is an expression of an opportunity for parallelism, not a command that mandates parallelism. The Intel Cilk Plus runtime will choose whether to run the function in parallel with its caller.

- `Cilk_sync`: Specifies that all spawned calls in a function must complete before execution continues. There is an implied cilk_sync at the end of every function that contains a cilk_spawn.

- `Cilk_for`: Allows iterations of the loop body to be executed in parallel.

The cilk_spawn and cilk_for keywords express opportunites for parallelism. Which portions of your application that actually run in parallel is determined by the Intel Cilk Plus runtime that implements task parallelism with an efficient work-stealing scheduler.

Reducers

Intel Cilk Plus includes *reducers* to help make parallel programming easier. Traditional parallel programs use locks to protect shared variables, which can be problematic. Incorrect lock use can result in deadlocks. Contention for locked regions of code can slow a program down. And while locks can prevent races, there is no way to enforce ordering, resulting in non-deterministic results. Reducers provide a lock-free mechanism that allows parallel code to use private "views" of a variable which are merged at the next sync. The merge is done in an ordered manner to maintain the serial semantics of the Intel Cilk Plus application.

Task Parallelism Tools

The Intel Cilk Plus SDK contains race detection and scalability analysis tools for Cilk-style parallelized binaries. The Cilk tools support code compiled with both the C/C++ compiler from the Intel Parallel Studio XE tool suites and the GCC "cilkplus" branch C/C++ compiler.

Array Notation

Intel Cilk Plus includes a set of notations that allow users to express high-level operations on entire arrays or sections of arrays. These notations help the compiler to effectively vectorize the application. Intel Cilk Plus allows C/C++ operations to be applied to multiple array elements in parallel, and also provides a set of builtin functions that can be used to perform vectorized shifts, rotates, and reductions.

SIMD-enabled Functions

A SIMD-enabled function is a regular function which can be invoked either on scalar arguments or on array elements in parallel. They are most useful when combined with array notation or `#pragma simd`.

#Pragma Simd

This pragma gives the compiler permission to vectorize a loop even in cases where auto-vectorization might fail. It is the simplest way to manually apply vectorization.

AspectC++

AspectC++ is an aspect-oriented extension of C and C++ languages. It has a source-to-source compiler, which translates AspectC++ source code into compilable C++. The compiler is available under the GNU GPL, though some extensions specific to Microsoft Windows are only available through pure-systems GmbH.

Aspect-oriented programming allows modularizing cross-cutting concerns in a single module, an aspect. Aspects can modify existing classes, but most commonly they provide 'advice' that runs before, after, or around existing functionality.

Example:

All calls to a specific function can be traced using an aspect, rather than inserting 'cerr' or print statements in many places:

```
aspect Tracer
{
    advice call("% %Iter::Reset(...)") : before()
    {
        cerr << "about to call Iter::Reset for " << JoinPoint::signature() << endl;
    }
};
```

The Tracer aspect will print out a message before any call to `%Iter::Reset`. The `%Iter` syntax means that it will match all classes that end in Iter.

Each 'matched' location in the source code is called a join point—the advice is joined to (or advises) that code. AspectC++ provides a join point API to provide and access to information about the join point. For example, the function:

```
JoinPoint::signature()
```

returns the name of the function (that matched `%Iter::Reset`) that is about to be called.

The join point API also provides compile-time type information that can be used within an aspect to access the type or the value of the arguments and the return type and return value of a method or function.

C++/CLI

C++/CLI (C++ modified for Common Language Infrastructure) is a language specification created by Microsoft and intended to supersede Managed Extensions for C++. It is a complete revision that aims to simplify the older Managed C++ syntax, which is now deprecated. C++/CLI was standardized by Ecma as ECMA-372. It is currently available in Visual Studio 2005, 2008, 2010, 2012, 2013, 2015, 2017 and 2019 including the Express editions.

C++/CLI is not mentioned in 'The .NET Language Strategy' by Mads Torgersen, posted February 1, 2017.

Syntax Changes

C++/CLI should be thought of as a language of its own (with a new set of keywords, for example), instead of the C++ superset-oriented Managed C++ (MC++) (whose non-standard keywords were styled like `__gc` or `__value`). Because of this, there are some major syntactic changes, especially related to the elimination of ambiguous identifiers and the addition of .NET-specific features.

Many conflicting syntaxes, such as the multiple versions of operator `new()` in MC++, have been split: in C++/CLI, .NET reference types are created with the new keyword `gcnew` (i.e. garbage collected new()). Also, C++/CLI has introduced the concept of generics from .NET (similar, for the most common purposes, to standard C++ templates, but quite different in their implementation).

Handles

In MC++, there were two different types of pointers: `__nogc` pointers were normal C++ pointers, while `__gc` pointers worked on .NET reference types. In C++/CLI, however, the only type of pointer is the normal C++ pointer, while the .NET reference types are accessed through a "handle", with the new syntax `ClassName^` (instead of `ClassName*`). This new construct is especially helpful when managed and standard C++ code is mixed; it clarifies which objects are under .NET automatic garbage collection and which objects the programmer must remember to explicitly destroy.

Tracking References

A tracking reference in C++/CLI is a handle of a passed-by-reference variable. It is similar in concept to using "`*&`" (reference to a pointer) in standard C++, and (in function declarations) corresponds to the "`ref`" keyword applied to types in C#, or "`ByRef`" in Visual Basic .NET. C++/CLI uses a "`^%`" syntax to indicate a tracking reference to a handle.

The following code shows an example of the use of tracking references. Replacing the tracking reference with a regular handle variable would leave the resulting string array with 10 uninitialized string handles, as only copies of the string handles in the array would be set, due to their being passed by value rather than by reference.

```
int main()
{
```

```
array<String^> ^arr = gcnew array<String^>(10);

int i = 0;


for each(String^% s in arr) {

    s = i++.ToString();

}


return 0;
```
}

This would be illegal in C#, which does not allow `foreach` loops to pass values by reference. Hence, a workaround would be required.

Finalizers and Automatic Variables

Another change in C++/CLI is the introduction of the finalizer syntax `!ClassName()`, a special type of nondeterministic destructor that is run as a part of the garbage collection routine. The C++ destructor syntax `~ClassName()` also exists for managed objects, and better reflects the "traditional" C++ semantics of deterministic destruction (that is, destructors that can be called by user code with `delete`).

In the raw .NET paradigm, the nondeterministic destruction model overrides the protected `Finalize` method of the root `Object` class, while the deterministic model is implemented through the `IDisposable` interface method `Dispose` (which the C++/CLI compiler turns the destructor into). Objects from C# or VB.NET code that override the Dispose method can be disposed of manually in C++/CLI with `delete` just as .NET classes in C++/CLI can.

```
// C++/CLI

ref class MyClass

{

public:

    MyClass();  // constructor

    ~MyClass(); // (deterministic) destructor (implemented as IDisposable.Dispose())

protected:

    !MyClass(); // finalizer (non-deterministic destructor) (implemented as Finalize())


public:

    static void Test()

    {
```

```
        MyClass automatic; // Not a handle, no initialization: compiler calls construc-
tor here


        MyClass ^user = gcnew MyClass();

        delete user;


        // Compiler calls automatic's destructor when automatic goes out of scope

    }

};
```

Operator Overloading

Operator overloading works analogously to standard C++. Every * becomes a ^, every & becomes an %, but the rest of the syntax is unchanged, except for an important addition: for .NET classes, operator overloading is possible not only for classes themselves, but also for references to those classes. This feature is necessary to give a ref class the semantics for operator overloading expected from .NET ref classes. (In reverse, this also means that for .NET framework ref classes, reference operator overloading often is implicitly implemented in C++/CLI.)

For example, comparing two distinct String references (String^) via the operator == will give true whenever the two strings are equal. The operator overloading is static, however. Thus, casting to Object^ will remove the overloading semantics.

```
//effects of reference operator overloading

String ^s1 = "abc";

String ^s2 = "ab" + "c";

Object ^o1 = s1;

Object ^o2 = s2;

s1 == s2; // true

o1 == o2; // false
```

C++/C# Interoperability

C++/CLI allows C++ programs to consume C# programs in C# DLLs. Here the #using keyword shows the compiler where the DLL is located for its compilation metadata. This simple example requires no data marshalling.

```
#include "stdafx.h"

using namespace System;

#using "...MyCS.dll"
```

```
int main(array<System::String ^> ^args) {

    double x = MyCS::Class1::add(40.1, 1.9);

    return 0;

}
```

The C# source code content of MyCS.DLL.

```
namespace MyCS {

    public class Class1 {

        public static double add(double a, double b) {

            return a + b;

        }

    }

}
```

This examples shows how strings are marshalled from C++ strings to strings callable from C# then back to C++ strings. String marshalling copies the string contents to forms usable in the different environments.

```
#include <string>

#include <iostream>

#include <msclr\marshal_cppstd.h>

#include "stdafx.h"

using namespace System;

#using "..MyCS.dll"


int main() {

        std::string s = "I am cat";

        System::String^ clrString = msclr::interop::marshal_as<System::String^>(s);  //
string usable from C#

        System::String^ t = MyCS::Class1::process(clrString); // call C# function

        std::string cppString = msclr::interop::marshal_as<std::string>(t); // string us-
able from C++

        std::cout << "Hello, C++/C# Interop!" << std::endl;

        std::cout << cppString << std::endl;

        return 0;

}
```

The C# code is not in any way C++-aware.

```
namespace MyCS {

    public class Class1 {
```

```
        public static string process(string a) {

            return a.Replace("cat", "dog") + " with a tail";

        }

    }

}
```

C++/C# interop allows C++ simplfied access to the entire world of .Net features.

The new C++/CX targeting WinRT, although it produces entirely unmanaged code, borrows the ref and ^ syntax for the reference-counted components of WinRT, which are similar to COM "objects".

C++/CX

C++/CX (C++ component extensions) is a language projection for Microsoft's Windows Runtime platform. It takes the form of a language extension for C++ compilers, and it enables C++ programmers to write programs that call Windows Runtime (WinRT) APIs. C++/CX is superseded by the C++/WinRT language projection, which is *not* an extension to the C++ language; rather, it's an entirely standard modern ISO C++17 header-file-based library.

The language extensions borrow syntax from C++/CLI but target the Windows Runtime Universal Windows Platform native code instead of the Common Language Runtime and managed code. It brings a set of syntax and library abstractions that project COM's WRL subset-based WinRT programming model in a way that is intuitive to C++/CLI managed extensions' coders.

It is possible to call the Windows Runtime from native ISO C++ via the lower level Windows Runtime C++ Template Library (WRL). However, WRL is also superseded by C++/WinRT.

Extension Syntax

C++/CX introduces syntax extensions for programming for the Windows Runtime. The overall non platform-specific syntax is compatible with the C++11 standard.

Objects

WinRT objects are created, or *activated*, using ref new and assigned to variables declared with the ^ (hat) notation inherited from C++/CLI.

```
Foo^ foo = ref new Foo();
```

A WinRT variable is simply a pair of a pointer to virtual method table and pointer to the object's internal data.

Reference Counting

A WinRT object is reference counted and thus handles similarly to ordinary C++ objects enclosed in shared_ptrs. An object will be deleted when there are no remaining references that lead to it.

There is no garbage collection involved. Nevertheless, the keyword `gcnew` has been reserved for possible future use.

Classes

Runtime Classes

There are special kinds of *runtime classes* that may contain component extension constructs. These are simply referred to as *ref classes* because they are declared using `ref class`.

```
public ref class MyClass

{


};
```

Partial Classes

C++/CX introduces the concept of partial classes. The feature allows a single class definition to be split across multiple files, mainly to enable the XAML graphical user interface design tools to auto-generate code in a separate file in order not to break the logic written by the developer. The parts are later merged at compilation.

.NET languages like C# have had this feature for many years. Partial classes have not yet made it into the C++ standard and cannot therefore be used in pure C++11.

A file that is generated and updated by the GUI-designer, and thus should not be modified by the programmer. Note the keyword `partial`.

```
// foo.private.h

#pragma once


partial ref class foo

{

private:

    int id_;

    Platform::String^ name_;

};
```

The file where the programmer writes user-interface logic. The header in which the compiler-generated part of the class is defined is imported. The keyword `partial` is not necessary.

```
// foo.public.h

#pragma once

#include "foo.private.h"
```

```
ref class foo

{

public:

    int GetId();

    Platform::String^ GetName();

};
```

This is the file in which the members of the partial class are implemented.

```
// foo.cpp

#include "pch.h"

#include "foo.public.h"


int foo::GetId() {return id_;}

Platform::String^ foo::GetName {return name_;}
```

Generics

Windows Runtime and thus C++/CX supports runtime-based generics. Generic type information is contained in the metadata and instantiated at runtime, unlike C++ templates which are compile-time constructs. Both are supported by the compiler and can be combined.

```
generic<typename T>

public ref class bag

{

    property T Item;

};
```

Metadata

All WinRT programs expose their declared classes and members through metadata. The format is the same that was standardized as part of the Common Language Infrastructure (CLI), the standard created from the .NET Framework. Because of this, code can be shared across C++/CX, CLI languages, and JavaScript that target Windows Runtime.

Runtime library

The C++/CX has a set of libraries that target the Windows Runtime. These help bridge the functionality of the C++ Standard Library and WinRT.

Preprocessor-based Detection

You can detect if C++/CX extension is turned on by testing existence of `__cplusplus_winrt` preprocessor symbol.

```
#ifdef __cplusplus_winrt

// C++/CX specific code goes here...

#endif
```

CUDA C/C++

CUDA C++ is just one of the ways you can create massively parallel applications with CUDA. It lets you use the powerful C++ programming language to develop high performance algorithms accelerated by thousands of parallel threads running on GPUs. Many developers have accelerated their computation- and bandwidth-hungry applications this way, including the libraries and frameworks that underpin the ongoing revolution in artificial intelligence known as Deep Learning.

So, you've heard about CUDA and you are interested in learning how to use it in your own applications. If you are a C or C++ programmer, this blog post should give you a good start. To follow along, you'll need a computer with an CUDA-capable GPU (Windows, Mac, or Linux, and any NVIDIA GPU should do), or a cloud instance with GPUs (AWS, Azure, IBM SoftLayer, and other cloud service providers have them).

```cpp
#include <iostream>

#include <math.h>


// function to add the elements of two arrays
void add(int n, float *x, float *y)
{
  for (int i = 0; i < n; i++)
      y[i] = x[i] + y[i];
}


int main(void)
{
  int N = 1<<20; // 1M elements

  float *x = new float[N];
  float *y = new float[N];
```

```
// initialize x and y arrays on the host
for (int i = 0; i < N; i++) {
  x[i] = 1.0f;
  y[i] = 2.0f;
}


// Run kernel on 1M elements on the CPU
add(N, x, y);


// Check for errors (all values should be 3.0f)
float maxError = 0.0f;
for (int i = 0; i < N; i++)
  maxError = fmax(maxError, fabs(y[i]-3.0f));
std::cout << "Max error: " << maxError << std::endl;


// Free memory
delete [] x;
delete [] y;


  return 0;
}
```

First, compile and run this C++ program. Put the code above in a file and save it as `add.cpp`, and then compile it with your C++ compiler. I'm on a Mac so I'm using `clang++`, but you can use `g++` on Linux or MSVC on Windows.

```
> clang++ add.cpp -o add
```

Then run it:

```
> ./add
 Max error: 0.000000
```

(On Windows you may want to name the executable add.exe and run it with `.\add`.)

As expected, it prints that there was no error in the summation and then exits. Now I want to get this computation running (in parallel) on the many cores of a GPU. It's actually pretty easy to take the first steps.

First, we just have to turn our `add` function into a function that the GPU can run, called a *kernel* in CUDA. To do this, all we have to do is add the specifier `__global__` to the function, which tells the CUDA C++ compiler that this is a function that runs on the GPU and can be called from CPU code.

```
// CUDA Kernel function to add the elements of two arrays on the GPU

__global__

void add(int n, float *x, float *y)

{

  for (int i = 0; i < n; i++)

    y[i] = x[i] + y[i];

}
```

These `__global__` functions are known as *kernels*, and code that runs on the GPU is often called device code, while code that runs on the CPU is *host code*.

Memory Allocation in CUDA

To compute on the GPU, we need to allocate memory accessible by the GPU. Unified Memory in CUDA makes this easy by providing a single memory space accessible by all GPUs and CPUs in your system. To allocate data in unified memory, call `cudaMallocManaged()`, which returns a pointer that you can access from host (CPU) code or device (GPU) code. To free the data, just pass the pointer to `cudaFree()`.

we just need to replace the calls to `new` in the code above with calls to `cudaMallocManaged()`, and replace calls to `delete []` with calls to `cudaFree`.

```
// Allocate Unified Memory -- accessible from CPU or GPU

  float *x, *y;

  cudaMallocManaged(&x, N*sizeof(float));

  cudaMallocManaged(&y, N*sizeof(float));


  ...


  // Free memory

  cudaFree(x);

  cudaFree(y);
```

Finally, we need to *launch* the `add()` kernel, which invokes it on the GPU. CUDA kernel launches are specified using the triple angle bracket syntax <<< >>>. we just have to add it to the call to `add` before the parameter list.

```
add<<<1, 1>>>(N, x, y);
```

We'll get into the details of what goes inside the angle brackets soon; for now all you need to know is that this line launches one GPU thread to run add().

Just one more thing: we need the CPU to wait until the kernel is done before it accesses the results (because CUDA kernel launches don't block the calling CPU thread). To do this we just call cudaDeviceSynchronize() before doing the final error checking on the CPU.

Here's the complete code:

```
#include <iostream>
#include <math.h>
// Kernel function to add the elements of two arrays
__global__
void add(int n, float *x, float *y)
{
  for (int i = 0; i < n; i++)
    y[i] = x[i] + y[i];
}


int main(void)
{
  int N = 1<<20;
  float *x, *y;


  // Allocate Unified Memory - accessible from CPU or GPU
  cudaMallocManaged(&x, N*sizeof(float));
  cudaMallocManaged(&y, N*sizeof(float));


  // initialize x and y arrays on the host
  for (int i = 0; i < N; i++) {
    x[i] = 1.0f;
    y[i] = 2.0f;
  }


  // Run kernel on 1M elements on the GPU
```

```
add<<<1, 1>>>(N, x, y);


    // Wait for GPU to finish before accessing on host
    cudaDeviceSynchronize();


    // Check for errors (all values should be 3.0f)
    float maxError = 0.0f;
    for (int i = 0; i < N; i++)
        maxError = fmax(maxError, fabs(y[i]-3.0f));
    std::cout << "Max error: " << maxError << std::endl;


    // Free memory
    cudaFree(x);
    cudaFree(y);


    return 0;
}
```

CUDA files have the file extension `.cu`. So save this code in a file called `add.cu` and compile it with `nvcc`, the CUDA C++ compiler.

```
> nvcc add.cu -o add_cuda
> ./add_cuda
Max error: 0.000000
```

This is only a first step, because as written, this kernel is only correct for a single thread, since every thread that runs it will perform the add on the whole array. Moreover, there is a race condition since multiple parallel threads would both read and write the same locations.

On Windows, you need to make sure you set Platform to x64 in the Configuration Properties for your project in Microsoft Visual Studio.

We think the simplest way to find out how long the kernel takes to run is to run it with `nvprof`, the command line GPU profiler that comes with the CUDA Toolkit. Just type `nvprof ./add_cuda` on the command line:

```
$ nvprof ./add_cuda
==3355== NVPROF is profiling process 3355, command: ./add_cuda
Max error: 0
```

```
==3355== Profiling application: ./add_cuda

==3355== Profiling result:

Time(%)      Time     Calls     Avg        Min        Max    Name

100.00%   463.25ms         1   463.25ms   463.25ms   463.25ms   add(int, float*, float*)

...
```

Above is the truncated output from `nvprof`, showing a single call to `add`. It takes about half a second on an NVIDIA Tesla K80 accelerator, and about the same time on an NVIDIA GeForce GT 740M in my 3-year-old Macbook Pro.

Let's make it faster with parallelism.

Picking up the Threads

Now that you've run a kernel with one thread that does some computation, how do you make it parallel? The key is in CUDA's `<<<1, 1>>>` syntax. This is called the execution configuration, and it tells the CUDA runtime how many parallel threads to use for the launch on the GPU. There are two parameters here, but let's start by changing the second one: the number of threads in a thread block. CUDA GPUs run kernels using blocks of threads that are a multiple of 32 in size, so 256 threads is a reasonable size to choose.

```
add<<<1, 256>>>(N, x, y);
```

If we run the code with only this change, it will do the computation once per thread, rather than spreading the computation across the parallel threads. To do it properly, I need to modify the kernel. CUDA C++ provides keywords that let kernels get the indices of the running threads. Specifically, `threadIdx.x` contains the index of the current thread within its block, and `blockDim.x` contains the number of threads in the block. I'll just modify the loop to stride through the array with parallel threads.

```
__global__
void add(int n, float *x, float *y)
{
  int index = threadIdx.x;
  int stride = blockDim.x;
  for (int i = index; i < n; i += stride)
      y[i] = x[i] + y[i];
}
```

The `add` function hasn't changed that much. In fact, setting `index` to 0 and `stride` to 1 makes it semantically identical to the first version.

Save the file as `add_block.cu` and compile and run it in `nvprof` again. For the remainder of the post we'll just show the relevant line from the output.

```
Time(%)        Time     Calls      Avg        Min        Max    Name

100.00%   2.7107ms         1   2.7107ms   2.7107ms   2.7107ms   add(int, float*, float*)
```

That's a big speedup (463ms down to 2.7ms), but not surprising since we went from 1 thread to 256 threads. The K80 is faster than my little Macbook Pro GPU (at 3.2ms). Let's keep going to get even more performance.

Out of the Blocks

CUDA GPUs have many parallel processors grouped into Streaming Multiprocessors, or SMs. Each SM can run multiple concurrent thread blocks. As an example, a Tesla P100 GPU based on the Pascal GPU Architecture has 56 SMs, each capable of supporting up to 2048 active threads. To take full advantage of all these threads, we should launch the kernel with multiple thread blocks.

By now you may have guessed that the first parameter of the execution configuration specifies the number of thread blocks. Together, the blocks of parallel threads make up what is known as the *grid*. Since we have N elements to process, and 256 threads per block, we just need to calculate the number of blocks to get at least N threads. We simply divide N by the block size (being careful to round up in case N is not a multiple of blockSize).

```
int blockSize = 256;

int numBlocks = (N + blockSize - 1) / blockSize;

add<<<numBlocks, blockSize>>>(N, x, y);
```

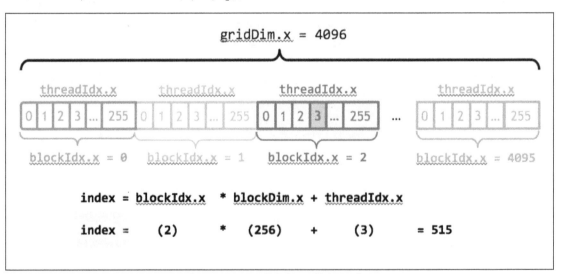

The CUDA parallel thread hierarchy.

CUDA executes kernels using a *grid* of *blocks* of *threads*. This figure shows the common indexing pattern used in CUDA programs using the CUDA keywords gridDim.x (the number of thread blocks), blockDim.x (the number of threads in each block), blockIdx.x (the index the current block within the grid), and threadIdx.x (the index of the current thread within the block).

We also need to update the kernel code to take into account the entire grid of thread blocks. CUDA provides `gridDim.x`, which contains the number of blocks in the grid, and `blockIdx.x`, which contains the index of the current thread block in the grid. figure illustrates the the approach to indexing into an array (one-dimensional) in CUDA using `blockDim.x`, `gridDim.x`, and `threadIdx.x`. The idea is that each thread gets its index by computing the offset to the beginning of its block (the block index times the block size: `blockIdx.x * blockDim.x`) and adding the thread's index within the block (`threadIdx.x`). The code `blockIdx.x * blockDim.x + threadIdx.x` is idiomatic CUDA.

```
__global__

void add(int n, float *x, float *y)

{

  int index = blockIdx.x * blockDim.x + threadIdx.x;

  int stride = blockDim.x * gridDim.x;

  for (int i = index; i < n; i += stride)

    y[i] = x[i] + y[i];

}
```

The updated kernel also sets `stride` to the total number of threads in the grid (`blockDim.x * gridDim.x`). This type of loop in a CUDA kernel is often called a *grid-stride loop*.

Save the file as `add_grid.cu` and compile and run it in `nvprof` again.

```
Time(%)      Time    Calls      Avg       Min       Max  Name

100.00%  94.015us        1  94.015us  94.015us  94.015us  add(int, float*, float*)
```

That's another 28x speedup, from running multiple blocks on all the SMs of a K80! We're only using one of the 2 GPUs on the K80, but each GPU has 13 SMs. Note the GeForce in my laptop has 2 (weaker) SMs and it takes 680us to run the kernel.

Managed Extensions for C++

For extending existing C++ applications with managed code, however, Managed C++ is a good choice. And if you plan to port an existing C++ application to run on the Framework, Managed C++ is also a good choice, since it saves you from rewriting large parts of your code. Although it's not as important in the .NET Framework world as either VB.NET or C#, Managed C++ is nevertheless a significant member of .NET's language arsenal. the convention defined in the ANSI standard for C++ extensions.) Among the most important of these are the following:

- `__gc`: Indicates that a type is subject to garbage collection. In other words, this keyword means that the type being declared is a CTS reference type. Managed C++ allows this keyword to be applied to classes, arrays, and other types.

- `__value`: Indicates that a type is not subject to garbage collection; that is, that the type is a CTS value type.

- `__interface`: Used to define a CTS interface type.

- `__box`: An operation that converts a CTS value type to a reference type.

- `__unbox`: An operation that converts a boxed CTS value type back to its original form.

- `__delegate`: Used to define a CTS delegate type.

A Managed C++ Example

C# and VB.NET were both designed for the CLR, while C++ was not. As a result, code written in Managed C++ can look a bit odd. Here's the same example this time in Managed C++:

```
// A Managed C++ example

# include "stdafx.h"

# using <mscorlib.dll>


__gc __interface IMath
{
   int Factorial(int f);
   double SquareRoot(double s);
};
__gc class Compute : public IMath
{
   public: int Factorial(int f)
   {
      int i;
      int result = 1;
      for (i=2; i<=f; i++)
          result = result * i;
      return result;
   };
   public: double SquareRoot(double s)
   {
      return System::Math::Sqrt(s);
   }
};
void main(void)
{
      Compute *c = new Compute;
```

```
int v;

v = 5;

System::Console::WriteLine("{0} factorial: {1}",
        __box(v), __box(c->Factorial(v)));

System::Console::WriteLine("Square root of {0}:
    {1:f4}",
        __box(v), __box(c->SquareRoot(v)));
}
```

The first thing to notice is how much this example resembles the C# version. Most of the basic syntax and many of the operators are the same. Yet it's different, too, beginning with the #include and #using statements necessary for creating managed code in C++. Following these, the interface IMath is defined, just as before. This time, however, it uses the __interface keyword and precedes it with the __gc keyword. The result is a C++ incarnation of a CTS-defined interface.

Next comes the class Compute, which implements the IMath interface. This class too is declared with the __gc keyword, which means that it's a CTS class with a lifetime managed by the CLR rather than the developer. The class varies a bit in syntax from the C# example, since C++ doesn't express things in exactly the same way, but it's nonetheless very similar.

The example ends with a standard C++ main function. Just like before, it creates an instance of the Compute class, then calls its two methods, all using standard C++ syntax. The only substantive difference is in the calls to WriteLine. Because this method expects reference parameters, the __box operator must be used to correctly pass the numeric parameters. Boxing also occurred for this parameter in C# and VB.NET, but it was done automatically. Because C++ was not originally built for the CLR, however, the developer must explicitly request this operation. Finally, just as you'd expect, the output of this example is the same as before: the factorial and square root of five.

Managed C++ Types

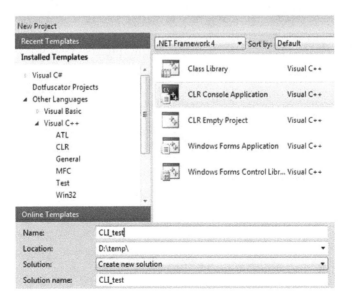

Managed C++ allows full access to the .NET Framework, including the types defined by the CLR and more. It's important to note that managed and unmanaged code, classes defined with and without __gc, can be defined in the same file, and they can exist in the same running process. Only the managed classes are subject to garbage collection, however; unmanaged classes must be explicitly freed as usual in C++. Table shows some of the major CLR types and their equivalents in Managed C++.

Other Managed C++ Features

Because it fully supports the CLR, there's much more in Managed C++. Delegates can be created using the __*delegate* keyword, while namespaces can be referenced with a *using namespace* statement, such as:

```
using namespace System;
```

Exceptions can be handled using try/catch blocks, and custom CLR exceptions can be created that inherit from System::Exception. Attributes can also be embedded in code using the same syntax as in C#.

Table: Some CLR Types and their Managed C++ Equivalents.

CLR	Managed C++
Byte	unsigned char
Char	wchar_t
Int16	short
Int32	int, long
Int64	__int64
UInt16	unsigned short
UInt32	unsigned int, unsigned long
UInt64	unsigned __int64
Single	float

Double	double
Decimal	Decimal
Boolean	bool
Structure	struct
String	String*
Class	__gc class
Interface	__gc __interface
Delegate	__delegate

Managed C++ is a major extension to the C++ environment provided by Visual Studio.NET, but it's not the only new feature. This latest edition of Microsoft's flagship development tool also includes better support for building traditional applications, including COM-based applications. Except for C++, all languages in Visual Studio.NET compile only to MSIL, and so require the .NET Framework to run. Since all Managed C++ classes are compiled to MSIL, the language can obviously be used to generate Framework-based code, but C++ is unique in that it also allows compiling directly to a machine-specific.

4

C++ Compilers

Software which is used to convert high-level programming language code into a low-level machine readable code is termed as a compiler. AMD optimizing C/C++ compiler, Clang, HP aC++, Intel C++ Compiler, Visual C++, etc. are some examples of the C++ compiler. The topics elaborated in this chapter will help in gaining a better perspective about the compilers in C++.

A compiler is a special program that processes statements written in a particular programming language and turns them into machine language or "code" that a computer's processor uses. Typically, a programmer writes language statements in a language such as Pascal or C one line at a time using an *editor*. The file that is created contains what are called the *source statements*. The programmer then runs the appropriate language compiler, specifying the name of the file that contains the source statements.

When executing (running), the compiler first parses (or analyzes) all of the language statements syntactically one after the other and then, in one or more successive stages or "passes", builds the output code, making sure that statements that refer to other statements are referred to correctly in the final code. Traditionally, the output of the compilation has been called object code or sometimes an object module .The object code is machine code that the processor can execute one instruction at a time.

The Java programming language, a language used in object-oriented programming, introduced the possibility of compiling output (called bytecode) that can run on any computer system platform for which a Java virtual machine or bytecode interpreter is provided to convert the bytecode into instructions that can be executed by the actual hardware processor. Using this virtual machine, the bytecode can optionally be recompiled at the execution platform by a just-in-time compiler.

Traditionally in some operating systems, an additional step was required after compilation - that of resolving the relative location of instructions and data when more than one object module was to be run at the same time and they cross-referred to each other's instruction sequences or data. This process was sometimes called *linkage editing* and the output known as a *load module*.

A compiler works with what are sometimes called 3GL and higher-level languages. An assembler works on programs written using a processor's assembler language.

AMD Optimizing C/C++ Compiler

The AMD Optimizing C/C++ Compiler (AOCC) is a free, open source, optimizing compiler from AMD targeting 32-bit and 64-bit Linux platforms. It is based on LLVM Clang 6.0 with various additional patches to improve performance for AMD's Ryzen microprocessors. AOCC also includes a version of DragonEgg gcc plugin for Fortran sources.

In a May 2017 benchmark comparing AOCC v1.0 to Clang 4 and 5, and GCC 6 through 8, Phoronix found AOCC provided significant but modest improvement over Clang 4.0 in several benchmarks and no difference in others. Compilation time generally increased relative to Clang 4.0. Some benchmarks found some versions of GCC had better performance than some versions of Clang (AOCC included), and vice versa.

Clang

Clang is a compiler front end for the C, C++, Objective-C and Objective-C++ programming languages, as well as the OpenMP, OpenCL, RenderScript and CUDA frameworks. It uses the LLVM compiler infrastructure as its back end and has been part of the LLVM release cycle since LLVM 2.6.

It is designed to act as a drop-in replacement for the GNU Compiler Collection (GCC), supporting most of its compilation flags and unofficial language extensions. Its contributors include Apple, Microsoft, Google, ARM, Sony, Intel and Advanced Micro Devices (AMD). It is open-source software, with source code released under the University of Illinois/NCSA License, a permissive free software licence. Since v9.0.0, it was relicensed to the Apache License 2.0 with LLVM Exceptions.

The Clang project includes the Clang front end, a static analyzer, and several code analysis tools.

Design

Clang is intended to work atop LLVM. The combination of Clang and LLVM provides most of the toolchain, to allow replacing the full GCC stack. Because it is built with a library-based design, like the rest of LLVM, Clang is easy to embed into other applications. This is one reason why most OpenCL implementations are built with Clang and LLVM.

One of Clang's main goals is to provide a library-based architecture, to allow the compiler to be more tightly tied to tools that interact with source code, such as an integrated development environment (IDE) graphical user interface (GUI). In contrast, GCC is designed to work in a compile-link-debug workflow, and integrating it with other tools is not always easy. For instance, GCC uses a step called *fold* that is key to the overall compile process, which has the side effect of translating the code tree into a form that looks unlike the original source code. If an error is found during or after the fold step, it can be difficult to translate that back into one location in the original source. Also, vendors using the GCC stack within IDEs use separate tools to index the code, to provide features like syntax highlighting and autocomplete.

Clang is designed to retain more information during the compiling process than GCC, and to preserve the overall form of the original code. The goal of this is to make it easier to map errors back into the original source. The error reports offered by Clang are also aimed to be more detailed and specific, as well as machine-readable, so IDEs can index the output of the compiler during compiling. Modular design of the compiler can offer source code indexing, syntax checking, and other features normally associated with rapid application development systems. The parse tree is also more suitable for supporting automated code refactoring, as it directly represents the original source code.

Clang compiles only C-like languages, such as C, C++, Objective-C, Objective-C++, OpenCL, and CUDA. For other languages, like Ada, LLVM remains dependent on GCC or another compiler frontend. In many cases, Clang can be used or swapped out for GCC as needed, with no other effects on the toolchain as a whole. It supports most of the commonly used GCC options. A sub-project *Flang* by Nvidia and The Portland Group added Fortran support.

Performance and GCC Compatibility

Clang is designed to be highly compatible with GCC. Clang's command-line interface is similar to and shares many flags and options with GCC. Clang implements many GNU language extensions and enables them by default. Clang implements many GCC compiler intrinsics purely for compatibility. For example, even though Clang implements atomic intrinsics which correspond exactly with C11 atomics, it also implements GCC's __sync_* intrinsics for compatibility with GCC and libstdc++. Clang also maintains ABI compatibility with GCC-generated object code. In practice Clang can often be used as a drop-in replacement for GCC.

Clang's developers aim to reduce memory footprint and increase compilation speed compared to competing compilers, such as GCC. In October 2007, they report that Clang compiled the Carbon libraries more than twice as fast as GCC, while using about one-sixth GCC's memory and disk space. However, as of 2011 this was not a typical result. As of mid-2014, Clang won more than a third of the benchmarks, with GCC winning most. As of 2014, performance of Clang-compiled programs lagged behind performance of the GCC-compiled program, sometimes by large factors (up to 5.5x), replicating earlier reports of slower performance.

More recent comparisons in November 2016 indicate that both compilers have evolved to increase their performance. As of GCC 4.8.2 versus clang 3.4, on a large harness of test files, GCC outperforms clang by approximately 17% on well-optimized source code. Test results are code-specific, and unoptimized C source code can reverse such differences. The two compilers now seem broadly comparable.

HP aC++

The HP C/aC++ Developer's Bundle includes the utilities for creating C and C++ programs. These tools provide features such as performance analysis, code analysis, and the HP-UX Developer's Toolkit. This product runs on HP-UX 11i v3, on the HP Integrity and HP 9000 systems.

Products

The HP C/aC++ Developer's Bundle includes:

- HP C/ANSI C compiler.

- HP aC++ compiler.

- HP-UX Developer's Toolkit.

- HP WDB debugger.

- HP Caliper performance analyser.

- HP Code Advisor (cadvise) analysis tool.

Intel C++ Compiler

Intel C++ Compiler, also known as icc or icl, is a group of C and C++ compilers from Intel available for Windows, Mac, Linux, FreeBSD and Intel-based Android devices.

The compilers generate optimized code for IA-32 and Intel 64 architectures, and non-optimized code for non-Intel but compatible processors, such as certain AMD processors. A specific release of the compiler (11.1) is available for development of Linux-based applications for IA-64 (Itanium 2) processors.

The 14.0 compiler added support for Intel-based Android devices and optimized vectorization and SSE Family instructions for performance. The 13.0 release added support for the Intel Xeon Phi coprocessor. It continues support for automatic vectorization, which can generate SSE, SSE2, SSE3, SSSE3, SSE4, AVX and AVX2 SIMD instructions, and the embedded variant for Intel MMX and MMX 2. Use of such instruction through the compiler can lead to improved application performance in some applications as run on IA-32 and Intel 64 architectures, compared to applications built with compilers that do not support these instructions.

Intel compilers support Cilk Plus, which is a capability for writing vectorized and parallel code that can be used on IA-32 and Intel 64 processors or which can be offloaded to Xeon Phi coprocessors. They also continue support for OpenMP 4.0, symmetric multiprocessing, automatic parallelization, and Guided Auto-Paralllization (GAP). With the add-on Cluster OpenMP capability, the compilers can also automatically generate Message Passing Interface calls for distributed memory multiprocessing from OpenMP directives.

Intel C++ is compatible with Microsoft Visual C++ on Windows and integrates into Microsoft Visual Studio. On Linux and Mac, it is compatible with GNU Compiler Collection (GCC) and the GNU toolchain. Intel C++ Compiler for Android is hosted on Windows, OS X or Linux and is compatible with the Android NDK, including gcc and the Eclipse IDE. Intel compilers are known for the application performance they can enable as measured by benchmarks, such as the SPEC CPU benchmarks.

Architectures

- IA-32.

- x86-64 (Intel 64 and AMD64).

- Intel Xeon Phi coprocessor.

- IA-64 (Itanium 2).

Packaging

Except for the Intel Bi-Endian C++ Compiler, Intel C++ compilers are not available in standalone form. They are available in suites:

- Intel Parallel Studio XE for development of technical, enterprise, and high-performance computing applications on Windows, Linux and Mac.

- Intel System Studio for development of system and app software for embedded systems or devices running Windows, Linux or Android.

The suites include other build tools, such as libraries, and tools for threading and performance analysis.

Flags and Manuals

Windows	Linux, macOS and FreeBSD	Comment
/Od	-O0	No optimization
/O1	-O1	Optimize for size
/O2	-O2	Optimize for speed and enable some optimization
/O3	-O3	Enable all optimizations as O2, and intensive loop optimizations
/arch:SSE3	/-msse3	Enables SSE3, SSE2 and SSE instruction sets optimizations for non-Intel CPUs
/fast	-fast	Shorthand. On Windows this equates to "/O3 /Qipo /QxHost /Opred-div-"; on Linux "-O3 -ipo -static -xHOST -no-prec-div". Note that the processor specific optimization flag (-xHOST) will optimize for the processor compiled on—it is the only flag of -fast that may be overridden
/Qprof-gen	-prof_gen	Compile the program and instrument it for a profile generating run
/Qprof-use	-prof_use	May only be used after running a program that was previously compiled using prof_gen. Uses profile information during each step of the compilation process

Debugging

The Intel compiler provides debugging information that is standard for the common debuggers (DWARF 2 on Linux, similar to gdb, and COFF for Windows). The flags to compile with debugging information are /Zi on Windows and -g on Linux. Debugging is done on Windows using the Visual Studio debugger and, on Linux, using gdb.

While the Intel compiler can generate a gprof compatible profiling output, Intel also provides a kernel level, system-wide statistical profiler called Intel VTune Amplifier. VTune can be used from a command line or thru an included GUI on Linux or Windows. It can also be integrated into Visual Studio on Windows, or Eclipse on Linux). In addition to the VTune profiler, there is Intel Advisor that specializes in vectorization optimization and tools for threading design and prototyping.

Intel also offers a tool for memory and threading error detection called Intel Inspector XE. Regarding memory errors, it helps detect memory leaks, memory corruption, allocation/de-allocation of API mismatches and inconsistent memory API usage. Regarding threading errors, it helps detect data races (both heap and stack), deadlocks and thread and synch API errors.

Visual C++

Microsoft Visual C++ (often abbreviated to MSVC) is an integrated development environment (IDE) product from Microsoft for the C, C++, and C++/CLI programming languages. MSVC is proprietary software; it was originally a standalone product but later became a part of Visual Studio and made available in both trialware and freeware forms. It features tools for developing and debugging C++ code, especially code written for the Windows API, DirectX and .NET.

Many applications require redistributable Visual C++ runtime library packages to function correctly. These packages are often installed independently of applications, allowing multiple applications to make use of the package while only having to install it once. These Visual C++ redistributable and runtime packages are mostly installed for standard libraries that many applications use.

The predecessor to Visual C++ was called *Microsoft C/C++*. There was also a *Microsoft QuickC* 2.5 and a *Microsoft QuickC for Windows* 1.0. The Visual C++ compiler is still known as *Microsoft C/C++* and as of the release of Visual C++ 2015 Update 2, is on version 19.00.23918.

16-bit Versions

- Microsoft C 1.0, based on Lattice C, was Microsoft's first C product in 1983. It was not K&R C.

- C 2.0 added large model support.

- C 3.0 was the first version developed inside Microsoft. This version intended compatibility with K&R and the later ANSI standard. It was being used inside Microsoft (for Windows and Xenix development) in early 1984. It shipped as a product in 1985.

- C 4.0 added optimizations and CodeView, a source-level debugger.

- C 5.0 added loop optimizations and 'huge memory model' (arrays bigger than 64k) support. Microsoft Fortran and the first 32 bit compiler for 80386 were also part of this project.

- C 5.1 released in 1988 allowed compiling programs for OS/2 1.x.

- C 6.0 released in 1989. It added global flow analysis, a source browser, and a new debugger, and included an optional C++ front end.

- C/C++ 7.0 was released in 1992. Added built-in support for C++ and MFC (Microsoft Foundation Class Library) 1.0.

- Visual C++ 1.0, which included MFC 2.0, was the first version of 'Visual' C++, released in February 1993. It was Cfront 2.1 compliant and available in two editions:

  ○ Standard: Replaced QuickC for Windows.

  ○ Professional: Replaced C/C++ 7.0. Included the ability to build both DOS and Windows applications, an optimizing compiler, a source profiler, and the Windows 3.1 SDK. The Phar Lap 286 DOS Extender Lite was also included.

- Visual C++ 1.5 was released in December 1993, included MFC 2.5, and added OLE 2.0 and ODBC support to MFC. It was the first version of Visual C++ that came only on CD-ROM.

  ○ Visual C++ 1.51 and 1.52 were available as part of a subscription service.

  ○ Visual C++ 1.52b is similar to 1.52, but does not include the Control Development Kit.

  ○ Visual C++ 1.52c was a patched version of 1.5. It is the last, and arguably most popular, development platform for Microsoft Windows 3.x. It is available through Microsoft Developer Network.

Strictly 32-bit Versions

- Visual C++ 1.0 (original name: Visual C++ 32-bit Edition) was the first version for 32-bit development for the Intel 386 architecture. Although released when 16-bit version 1.5 was available, it did not include support for OLE2 and ODBC. It was also available in a bundle called Visual C++ 16/32-bit Suite, which included Visual C++ 1.5.

- Visual C++ 2.0, which included MFC 3.0, was the first version to be 32-bit only. In many ways, this version was ahead of its time, since Windows 95, then codenamed "Chicago", was not yet released, and Windows NT had only a small market share. Microsoft included and updated Visual C++ 1.5 as part of the 2.x releases up to 2.1, which included Visual C++ 1.52, and both 16-bit and 32-bit version of the Control Development Kit (CDK) were included. Visual C++ 2.x also supported Win32s development. It is available through Microsoft Developer Network. There was a Visual C++ 2.0 RISC Edition for MIPS and Alpha processors, as well as a cross-platform edition for the Macintosh (68000 instruction set).

  ○ Visual C++ 2.1 and 2.2 were updates for 2.0 available through subscription.

- Visual C++ 4.0, released on 1995-12-11, introduced the Developer Studio IDE. Its then-novel tiled layout of non-overlapping panels—navigation panel, combination editor/source level debugger panel, and console output panel—continues through the Visual Studio product line (as of 2013). Visual C++ 4.0 included MFC 4.0, was designed for Windows 95 and Windows NT. To allow support of legacy (Windows 3.x/DOS) projects, 4.0 came bundled with the Visual C++ 1.52 installation CD. Updates available through subscription included Visual C++ 4.1, which came with the Microsoft Game SDK (later released separately as the

DirectX SDK), and Visual C++ 4.2. Version number 3.0 was skipped to achieve version number parity between Visual C++ 4.0 and MFC 4.0.

- Visual C++ 4.2 did not support Windows 3.x (Win32s) development. This was the final version with a cross-platform edition for the Macintosh available and it differed from the 2.x version in that it also allowed compilation for the PowerPC instruction set.

- Visual C++ 5.0, which included MFC 4.21 and was released 1997-04-28, was a major upgrade from 4.2. Available in four editions: Learning, Professional, Enterprise, and RISC.

- Visual C++ 6.0 (commonly known as VC6), which included MFC 6.0, was released in 1998. The release was somewhat controversial since it did not include an expected update to MFC. Visual C++ 6.0 is still quite popular and often used to maintain legacy projects. There are, however, issues with this version under Windows XP, especially under the debugging mode (for example, the values of static variables do not display). The debugging issues can be solved with a patch called the "Visual C++ 6.0 Processor Pack". Version number: 12.00.8804

- Visual C++ .NET 2002 (also known as Visual C++ 7.0), which included MFC 7.0, was released in 2002 with support for link time code generation and debugging runtime checks, .NET 1.0, and Visual C# and Managed C++. The new user interface used many of the hot keys and conventions of Visual Basic, which accounted for some of its unpopularity among C++ developers. Version number: 13.00.9466

- Visual C++ .NET 2003 (also known as Visual C++ 7.1), which included MFC 7.1, was released in 2003 along with .NET 1.1 and was a major upgrade to Visual C++ .NET 2002. It was considered a patch to Visual C++ .NET 2002. Accordingly, the English language upgrade version of Visual Studio .NET 2003 shipped for minimal cost to owners of the English-language version of Visual Studio .NET 2002. This was the last version to support Windows 95 and NT 4.0 as a target. Version number: 13.10.3077

- eMbedded Visual C++ in various versions was used to develop for some versions of the Windows CE operating system. Initially it replaced a development environment consisting of tools added onto Visual C++ 6.0. eMbedded Visual C++ was replaced as a separate development environment by Microsoft Visual Studio 2005.

32-bit and 64-bit Versions

- Visual C++ 2005 (also known as Visual C++ 8.0), which included MFC 8.0, was released in November 2005. This version supports .NET 2.0 and includes a new version of C++ targeted to the .NET framework (C++/CLI) with the purpose of replacing the previous version (Managed C++). Managed C++ for CLI is still available via compiler options, though. It also introduced OpenMP. With Visual C++ 2005, Microsoft also introduced Team Foundation Server. Visual C++ 8.0 has problems compiling MFC AppWizard projects that were created using Visual Studio 6.0, so maintenance of legacy projects can be continued with the original IDE if rewriting is not feasible. Visual C++ 2005 is the last version able to target Windows 98 and Windows Me. SP1 version (14.00.50727.762) is also available in Microsoft Windows SDK Update for Windows Vista.

- Visual C++ 2008 (also known as Visual C++ 9.0) was released in November 2007. This version supports .NET 3.5. Managed C++ for CLI is still available via compiler options. By default, all applications compiled against the Visual C++ 2008 Runtimes (static and dynamic linking) will only work under Windows 2000 and later. A feature pack released for VC9, later included in SP1, added support for C++ TR1 library extensions. SP1 version (15.00.30729.01) is also available in Microsoft Windows SDK for Windows 7.

- Some versions of Visual C++ supported Itanium 2.

- Visual C++ 2010 (also known as Visual C++ 10.0) was released on April 12, 2010. It uses a SQL Server Compact database to store information about the source code, including IntelliSense information, for better IntelliSense and code-completion support. However, Visual C++ 2010 does not support Intellisense for C++/CLI. This version adds a C++ parallel computing library called the Parallel Patterns Library, partial support for C++11, significantly improved IntelliSense based on the Edison Design Group front end, and performance improvements to both the compiler and generated code. This version is built on .NET 4.0, but supports compiling to machine code. The partial C++11 support mainly consists of six compiler features: lambdas, rvalue references, auto, decltype, static_assert, and nullptr. C++11 also supports library features (e.g., moving the TR1 components from std::tr1 namespace directly to std namespace). Variadic templates were also considered, but delayed until some future version due to having a lower priority, which stemmed from the fact that, unlike other costly-to-implement features (lambda, rvalue references), variadic templates would benefit only a minority of library writers rather than the majority of compiler end users. By default, all applications compiled against Visual C++ 2010 Runtimes only work on Windows XP SP2 and later. The RTM version (16.00.30319) is also available in Windows SDK for Windows 7 and .NET Framework 4 (WinSDK v7.1). SP1 version (16.00.40219) is available as part of Visual Studio 2010 Service Pack 1 or through the Microsoft Visual C++ 2010 Service Pack 1 Compiler Update for the Windows SDK 7.1.

- Visual C++ 2012 (also known as Visual C++ 11.0) was released on August 15, 2012. It features improved C++11 support, and support for Windows Runtime development.]

- Visual C++ 2013 (also known as Visual C++ 12.0) was released on October 17, 2013. It features further C++11 and C99 support, and introduces a REST SDK.

- Visual C++ 2015 (also known as Visual C++ 14.0) was released on July 20, 2015. It features improved C++11/14/17 support. Without any announcement from Microsoft, Visual Studio 2015 Update 2 started generating telemetry calls in compiled binaries. After some users contacted Microsoft about this problem, Microsoft said they would remove these telemetry calls when compiling with the future Visual Studio 2015 Update 3. The function in question was removed from the Visual C++ CRT static libraries in Visual Studio 2015 Update 3.

- Visual C++ 2017 (also known as Visual C++ 14.1) was released on March 7, 2017.

- Visual C++ 2019 (also known as Visual C++ 14.2) was released on April 2, 2019.

Internal Version Numbering

The predefined macro _MSC_VER indicates the major and minor version numbers of the Visual C++

compiler. The macro's value is an integer literal in which the last two digits indicate the minor version number and the preceding digits indicate the major version number.

From Visual Studio 2017, _MSC_VER is incremented monotonically at every Visual C++ toolset update. Thus, for example, the version of MSVC++ 14.1 that ships with Visual Studio 2017 version 15.3.0 sets _MSC_VER to 1911. Microsoft recommends using the >= operator to test the value of _MSC_VER.

Here are values of _MSC_VER for various versions of the Visual C++ compiler:

```
MSC     1.0     _MSC_VER == 100

MSC     2.0     _MSC_VER == 200

MSC     3.0     _MSC_VER == 300

MSC     4.0     _MSC_VER == 400

MSC     5.0     _MSC_VER == 500

MSC     6.0     _MSC_VER == 600

MSC     7.0     _MSC_VER == 700

MSVC++ 1.0     _MSC_VER == 800

MSVC++ 2.0     _MSC_VER == 900

MSVC++ 4.0     _MSC_VER == 1000 (Developer Studio 4.0)

MSVC++ 4.2     _MSC_VER == 1020 (Developer Studio 4.2)

MSVC++ 5.0     _MSC_VER == 1100 (Visual Studio 97 version 5.0)

MSVC++ 6.0     _MSC_VER == 1200 (Visual Studio 6.0 version 6.0)

MSVC++ 7.0     _MSC_VER == 1300 (Visual Studio .NET 2002 version 7.0)

MSVC++ 7.1     _MSC_VER == 1310 (Visual Studio .NET 2003 version 7.1)

MSVC++ 8.0     _MSC_VER == 1400 (Visual Studio 2005 version 8.0)

MSVC++ 9.0     _MSC_VER == 1500 (Visual Studio 2008 version 9.0)

MSVC++ 10.0    _MSC_VER == 1600 (Visual Studio 2010 version 10.0)

MSVC++ 11.0    _MSC_VER == 1700 (Visual Studio 2012 version 11.0)

MSVC++ 12.0    _MSC_VER == 1800 (Visual Studio 2013 version 12.0)

MSVC++ 14.0    _MSC_VER == 1900 (Visual Studio 2015 version 14.0)

MSVC++ 14.1    _MSC_VER == 1910 (Visual Studio 2017 version 15.0)

MSVC++ 14.11   _MSC_VER == 1911 (Visual Studio 2017 version 15.3)

MSVC++ 14.12   _MSC_VER == 1912 (Visual Studio 2017 version 15.5)

MSVC++ 14.13   _MSC_VER == 1913 (Visual Studio 2017 version 15.6)

MSVC++ 14.14   _MSC_VER == 1914 (Visual Studio 2017 version 15.7)
```

```
MSVC++ 14.15 _MSC_VER == 1915 (Visual Studio 2017 version 15.8)

MSVC++ 14.16 _MSC_VER == 1916 (Visual Studio 2017 version 15.9)

MSVC++ 14.2  _MSC_VER == 1920 (Visual Studio 2019 Version 16.0)

MSVC++ 14.21 _MSC_VER == 1921 (Visual Studio 2019 Version 16.1)

MSVC++ 14.22 _MSC_VER == 1922 (Visual Studio 2019 Version 16.2)

MSVC++ 14.23 _MSC_VER == 1923 (Visual Studio 2019 Version 16.3)
```

These version numbers refer to the major version number of the Visual C++ compilers and libraries, as can be seen from the installation directories. It does not refer to the year in the name of the Visual Studio release. A thorough list is available.

Compatibility

ABI

The Visual C++ compiler ABI have historically changed between major compiler releases. This is especially the case for STL containers, where container sizes have varied a lot between compiler releases. Microsoft therefore recommends against using C++ interfaces at module boundaries when one wants to enable client code compiled using a different compiler version. Instead of C++, Microsoft recommends using C or COM interfaces, which are designed to have a stable ABI between compiler releases.

C runtime Libraries

Visual C++ ships with different versions of C runtime libraries. This means users can compile their code with any of the available libraries. However, this can cause some problems when using different components (DLLs, EXEs) in the same program. A typical example is a program using different libraries. The user should use the same C Run-Time for all the program's components unless the implications are understood. Microsoft recommends using the multithreaded, dynamic link library (/MD or /MDd compiler option) to avoid possible problems.

C

Although the product originated as an IDE for the C programming language, for many years the compiler's support for that language conformed only to the original edition of the C standard, dating from 1989, but not the C99 revision of the standard.

Visual C++ 2013 finally added support for various C99 features in its C mode (including designated initializers, compound literals, and the `_Bool` type), though it was still not complete. Visual C++ 2015 further improved the C99 support, with full support of the C99 Standard Library, except for features that require C99 language features not yet supported by the compiler.

Most of the changes from the C11 revision of the standard are still not supported by Visual C++ 2017. For example, generic selections via the `_Generic` keyword are not supported by the compiler and result in a syntax error.

Full C11 conformance is on our roadmap, and updating the preprocessor is just the first step in that process. The C11 _Generic feature is not actually part of the preprocessor, so it has not yet been implemented. When implemented we expect the feature to work independent of if the traditional or updated preprocessor logic is used.

5
Algorithms in C++

An algorithm is a piece of code which takes input from the user and produces a desirable output. It uses a set of rules and protocols for performing calculations and solving a problem. Heap sort, merge sort, quick sort, radix sort, bubble sort, etc. are some of the algorithms used in C++. This chapter closely examines these C++ algorithms to provide an extensive understanding of the subject.

In C++, the designation identifies a group of functions that run on a designated range of elements. The algorithms are used to solve problems or provide functionality. Algorithms work exclusively on values; they don't affect the size or storage of a container. Simple algorithms can be implemented within a function. Complex algorithms might require several functions or even a class to implement them.

Classifications and Examples of Algorithms in C++

The classifications of algorithms with a few examples are:

- Sorting (sort, partial sort, nth_element).

- Binary Search (lower_bound, upper_bound).

- Partitions (partition, partition_copy).

- Merge (includes, set_intersection, merge).

- Heap (make_heap, push_heap).

Search Algorithms - Linear Search and Binary Search

Linear Search

The most obvious algorithm is to start at the beginning and walk to the end, testing for a match at each item:

```
bool jw_search ( int *list, int size, int key, int*& rec )
{
```

```
// Basic sequential search
bool found = false;
int i;


for ( i = 0; i < size; i++ ) {
  if ( key == list[i] )
    break;
}
if ( i < size ) {
  found = true;
  rec = &list[i];
}


return found;
}
```

This algorithm has the benefit of simplicity; it is difficult to get wrong, unlike other more sophisticated solutions. The above code follows the following convention:

- All search routines return a true/false boolean value for success or failure.

- The list will be either an array of integers or a linked list of integers with a key.

- The found item will be saved in a reference to a pointer for use in client code.

The algorithm itself is simple. A familiar 0 - n-1 loop to walk over every item in the array, with a test to see if the current item in the list matches the search key. The loop can terminate in one of two ways. If i reaches the end of the list, the loop condition fails. If the current item in the list matches the key, the loop is terminated early with a break statement. Then the algorithm tests the index variable to see if it is less that size (thus the loop was terminated early and the item was found), or not (and the item was not found).

For a linked list defined as:

```
struct node {
  int rec;
  int key;
  node *next;


  node ( int r, int k, node *n )
    : rec ( r )
```

```
    , key ( k )

    , next ( n )

  { }

};
```

The algorithm is equally simple:

```
bool jw_search ( node*& list, int key, int*& rec )

{

  // Basic sequential search

  bool found = false;

  node *i;


  for ( i = list; i != 0; i = i->next ) {

    if ( key == i->key )

      break;

  }

  if ( i != 0 ) {

    found = true;

    rec = &i->rec;

  }


  return found;

}
```

Instead of a counting loop, we use an idiom for walking a linked list The loop terminates if i is a null pointer (the algorithm assumes a null pointer terminates the list) or if the item was found.

The basic sequential search algorithm can be improved in a number of ways. One of those ways is to assume that the item being searched for will always be in the list. This way you can avoid the two termination conditions in the loop in favor of only one. Of course, that creates the problem of a failed search. If we assume that the item will always be found, how can we test for failure?

The answer is to use a list that is larger in size than the number of items by one. A list with ten items would be allocated a size of eleven for use by the algorithm. The concept is much like C-style strings and the nul terminator. The nul character has no practical use except as a dummy item delimiting the end of the string. When the algorithm starts, we can simply place the search key in list[size] to ensure that it will always be found:

```
bool jw_search ( int *list, int size, int key, int*& rec )
```

```
{
  // Quick sequential search

  bool found = false;

  int i;


  list[size] = key;

  for ( i = 0; key != list[i]; i++ )

    ;

  if ( i < size ) {

    found = true;

    rec = &list[i];

  }


  return found;

}
```

The only test in the traversal loop is testing for a match. We know that the item is in the list somewhere, so there's no need for a loop body. After the loop the algorithm simply tests if i is less than size. If it is then we have found a real match, otherwise i is equal to size. Because list[-size] is where the dummy item was, we can safely say that the item does not exist anywhere else in the list. This algorithm is faster because it reduces two tests in the loop to one test. It isn't a big improvement, but if jw_search is called often on large lists, the optimization may become noticeable.

Another variation of sequential search assumes that the list is ordered (in ascending sorted order for the algorithm we will use):

```
bool jw_search ( int *list, int size, int key, int*& rec )

{
  // Ordered sequential search

  bool found = false;

  int i;


  for ( i = 0; i < size && key > list[i]; i++ )

    ;

  if ( key == list[i] ) {

    found = true;
```

```
      rec = &list[i];

  }


  return found;

}
```

The performance for a successful search where all keys are equally likely is the same as the basic algorithm. The speed improvement is for failed searches. Because the absence of an item can be determined more quickly, the average speed of a failed search is twice that of previous algorithms on average. By combining the Quick sequential search and the Ordered sequential search, one can have a highly tuned sequential search algorithm.

Self Organizing Search

For lists that do not have a set order requirement, a self organizing algorithm may be more efficient if some items in the list are searched for more frequently than others. By bubbling a found item toward the front of the list, future searches for that item will be executed more quickly. This speed improvement takes advantage of the fact that 80% of all operations are performed on 20% of the items in a data set. If those items are nearer to the front of the list then search will be sped up considerably.

The first solution that comes to mind is to move the found item to the front. With an array this would result in rather expensive memory shifting:

```
bool jw_search ( int *list, int size, int key, int*& rec )

{

  // Self-organizing (move to front) search

  bool found = false;


  // Is it already at the front?

  if ( key == list[0] ) {

    rec = &list[0];

    found = true;

  }

  else {

    int i;

    for ( i = 1; i < size; i++ ) {

      if ( key == list[i] )

        break;
```

```
  }

  if ( i < size ) {
    int save = list[i];
    // Fill the hole left by list[i]
    for ( int j = i; j < size - 1; j++ )
      list[j] = list[j + 1];
    // Make room at the front
    for ( int j = size - 1; j > 0; j-- )
      list[j] = list[j - 1];
    list[0] = save;
    rec = &list[0];
    found = true;
  }

}


  return found;

}
```

Filling the hole left by removing the found item and then shifting the entire contents of the array to make room at the front is dreadfully expensive and probably would make this algorithm impractical for arrays. However, with a linked list the splicing operation required to restructure the list and send the item to the front is quick and trivial:

```
bool jw_search ( node*& list, int key, int*& rec )

{

  // Self-organizing (move to front) search

  node *iter = list;

  bool found = false;


  // Is it already at the front?

  if ( key == iter->key ) {

    rec = &iter->rec;

    found = true;

  }

  else {
```

```
    for ( ; iter->next != 0; iter = iter->next ) {

      if ( key == iter->next->key )

        break;

    }

    // Was the item found?

    if ( iter->next != 0 ) {

      // Remove the node and fix the list

      node *save = iter->next;

      iter->next = save->next;

      // Place the node at the front

      save->next = list;

      list = save;

      rec = &list->rec;

      found = true;

    }

  }


  return found;

}
```

For a linked data structure, moving an item to a new position over large distances has a constant time complexity, O(1), whereas for contiguous memory such as an array, the time complexity is O(N) where N is the range of items being shifted. A solution that is just as effective, but takes longer to reach the optimal limit is to swap the found item with the previous item in the list. This algorithm is where arrays excel over linked lists for our data set of integers. The cost of swapping two integers is less than that of surgery with pointers. The code is simple as well:

```
bool jw_search ( int *list, int size, int key, int*& rec )

{

  // Self-organizing (swap with previous) search

  bool found = false;

  int i;


  for ( i = 0; i < size; i++ ) {

    if ( key == list[i] )

      break;
```

```
  }
  // Was it found?
  if ( i < size ) {
    // Is it already the first?
    if ( i > 0 ) {
      int save = list[i - 1];
      list[i - 1] = list[i];
      list[i--] = save;
    }
    found = true;
    rec = &list[i];
  }


  return found;
}
```

Binary Search

All of the sequential search algorithms have the same problem; they walk over the entire list. Some of our improvements work to minimize the cost of traversing the whole data set, but those improvements only cover up what is really a problem with the algorithm. By thinking of the data in a different way, we can make speed improvements that are much better than anything sequential search can guarantee.

Consider a list in ascending sorted order. It would work to search from the beginning until an item is found or the end is reached, but it makes more sense to remove as much of the working data set as possible so that the item is found more quickly. If we started at the middle of the list we could determine which half the item is in (because the list is sorted). This effectively divides the working range in half with a single test. By repeating the procedure, the result is a highly efficient search algorithm called binary search.

The actual algorithm is surprisingly tricky to implement considering the apparent simplicity of the concept. Here is a correct function that implements binary search by marking the current lower and upper bounds for the working range:

```
bool jw_search ( int *list, int size, int key, int*& rec )
{
  // Binary search
  bool found = false;
  int low = 0, high = size - 1;
```

```
while ( high >= low ) {

  int mid = ( low + high ) / 2;

  if ( key < list[mid] )

    high = mid - 1;

  else if ( key > list[mid] )

    low = mid + 1;

  else {

    found = true;

    rec = &list[mid];

    break;

  }

}


  return found;

}
```

Readers are expected to trace its execution on paper and with a test program to fully understand its elegance. Binary search is very efficient, but it can be improved by writing a variation that searches more like humans do. Consider how you would search for a name in the phonebook. They would begin at the most likely location and then use that location as a gauge for the next most likely location. Such a search is called interpolation search because it estimates the position of the item being searched for based on the upper and lower bounds of the range. The algorithm itself isn't terribly difficult, but it does seem that way with the range calculation:

```
bool jw_search ( int *list, int size, int key, int*& rec )

{

  // Interpolation search

  bool found = false;

  int low = 0, high = size - 1;


  while ( list[high] >= key && key > list[low] ) {

    double low_diff = (double)key - list[low];

    double range_diff = (double)list[high] - list[low];

    double count_diff = (double)high - low;

    int range = (int)( low_diff / range_diff * count_diff + low );

    if ( key > list[range] )
```

```
     low = range + 1;

   else if ( key < list[range] )

     high = range - 1;

   else

     low = range;

 }

 if ( key == list[low] ) {

   found = true;

   rec = &list[low];

 }


 return found;

}
```

Interpolation search is theoretically superior to binary search. With an average time complexity of O(log log n), interpolation search beats binary search's O(log n) easily. However, tests have shown that interpolation search isn't significantly better in practice unless the data set is very large. Otherwise, binary search is faster.

Heap Sort

Heapsort is one of the most efficient sorting techniques. This technique builds a heap from the given unsorted array and then uses the heap again to sort the array.

Heapsort is a sorting technique based on comparison and uses binary heap.

Binary Heap

A binary heap is represented using a complete binary tree. A complete binary tree is a binary tree in which all the nodes at each level are completely filled except for the leaf nodes and the nodes are as far as left.

A binary heap or simply a heap is a complete binary tree where the items or nodes are stored in a way such that the root node is greater than its two child nodes. This is also called max heap.

The items in the binary heap can also be stored as min-heap wherein the root node is smaller than its two child nodes. We can represent a heap as a binary tree or an array.

While representing a heap as an array, assuming the index starts at 0, the root element is stored at 0. In general, if a parent node is at the position I, then the left child node is at the position (2*I + 1) and the right node is at (2*I +2).

General Algorithm

Given below is the general algorithm for heap sort technique:

- Build a max heap from the given data such that the root is the highest element of the heap.
- Remove the root i.e. the highest element from the heap and replace or swap it with the last element of the heap.
- Then adjust the max heap, so as to not to violate the max heap properties (heapify).
- The above step reduces the heap size by 1.
- Repeat the above three steps until the heap size is reduced to 1.

As shown in the general algorithm to sort the given dataset in increasing order, we first construct a max heap for the given data.

Let us take an example to construct a max heap with the following dataset: 6, 10, 2, 4, 1

We can construct a tree for this data set as follows.

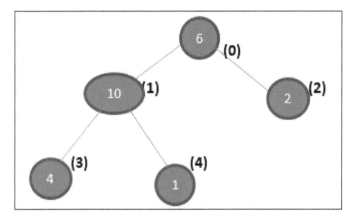

In the above tree representation, the numbers in the brackets represent the respective positions in the array.

In order to construct a max heap of the above representation, we need to fulfill the heap condition that the parent node should be greater than its child nodes. In other words, we need to "heapify" the tree so as to convert it to max-heap.

After heapification of the above tree, we will get the max-heap as shown below.

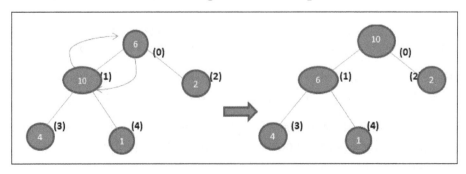

As shown above, we have this max-heap generated from an array.

Next, we present an illustration of a heap sort. Having seen the construction of max-heap, we will skip the detailed steps to construct a max-heap and will directly show the max heap at each step.

Consider the following array of elements. We need to sort this array using the heap sort technique.

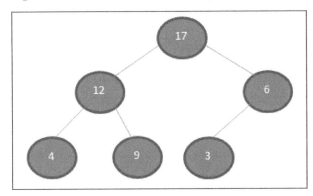

Let us construct a max-heap as shown below for the array to be sorted.

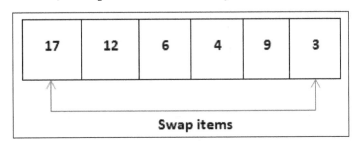

Once the heap is constructed, we represent it in an Array form as shown below.

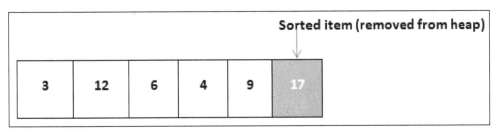

Now we compare the 1st node (root) with the last node and then swap them. Thus, as shown above, we swap 17 and 3 so that 17 is at the last position and 3 is in the first position.

Now we remove the node 17 from the heap and put it in the sorted array as shown in the shaded portion below.

Now we again construct a heap for the array elements. This time the heap size is reduced by 1 as we have deleted one element (17) from the heap.

The heap of the remaining elements is shown below.

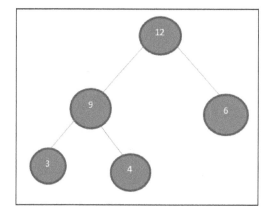

In the next step, we will repeat the same steps.

We compare and swap the root element and last element in the heap.

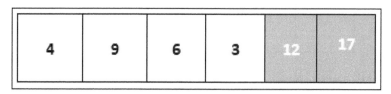

After swapping, we delete the element 12 from the heap and shift it to the sorted array.

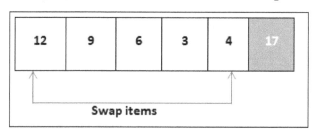

Once again we construct a max heap for the remaining elements as shown below.

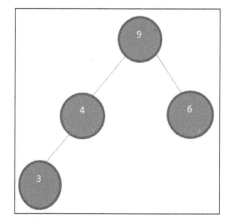

Now we swap the root and the last element i.e. 9 and 3. After swapping, element 9 is deleted from the heap and put in a sorted array.

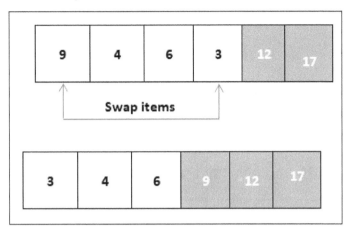

At this point, we have only three elements in the heap as shown below.

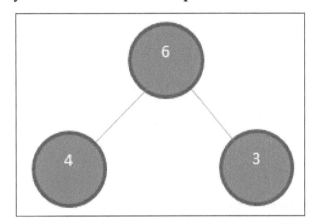

We swap 6 and 3 and delete the element 6 from the heap and add it to the sorted array.

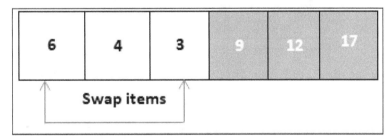

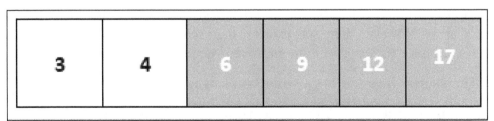

Now we construct a heap of the remaining elements and then swap both with each other.

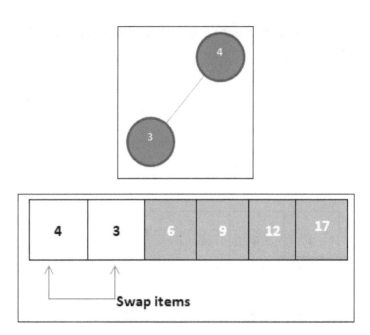

After swapping 4 and 3, we delete element 4 from the heap and add it to the sorted array. Now we have only one node remaining in the heap as shown below.

So now with only one node remaining, we delete it from the heap and add it to the sorted array.

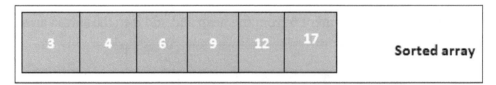

Thus the above shown is the sorted array that we have obtained as a result of the heap sort.

In the above illustration, we have sorted the array in ascending order. If we have to sort the array in descending order then we need to follow the same steps but with the min-heap.

Heapsort algorithm is identical to selection sort in which we select the smallest element and place it into a sorted array. However, heap sort is faster than selection sort as far as the performance is concerned. We can put it as heapsort is an improved version of the selection sort.

Next, we will implement Heapsort in C++ and Java language.

The most important function in both the implementations is the function "heapify". This function is called by the main heapsort routine to rearrange the subtree once a node is deleted or when max-heap is built.

When we have heapified the tree correctly, only then we will be able to get the correct elements in their proper positions and thus the array will be correctly sorted.

C++ Example

Following is the C++ code for heapsort implementation:

```cpp
#include <iostream>

using namespace std;


// function to heapify the tree
void heapify(int arr[], int n, int root)
{

    int largest = root; // root is the largest element

    int l = 2*root + 1; // left = 2*root + 1

    int r = 2*root + 2; // right = 2*root + 2


    // If left child is larger than root

    if (l < n && arr[l] > arr[largest])


    largest = l;


    // If right child is larger than largest so far

    if (r < n && arr[r] > arr[largest])

    largest = r;


    // If largest is not root

    if (largest != root)

        {

        //swap root and largest

        swap(arr[root], arr[largest]);


        // Recursively heapify the sub-tree

        heapify(arr, n, largest);

        }
```

```
}


// implementing heap sort
void heapSort(int arr[], int n)
{
    // build heap
    for (int i = n / 2 - 1; i >= 0; i--)
    heapify(arr, n, i);


    // extracting elements from heap one by one
    for (int i=n-1; i>=0; i--)
    {
        // Move current root to end
        swap(arr[0], arr[i]);


        // again call max heapify on the reduced heap
        heapify(arr, i, 0);
    }
}


/* print contents of array - utility function */
void displayArray(int arr[], int n)
{
    for (int i=0; i<n; ++i)
    cout << arr[i] << " ";
    cout << "\n";
}


// main program
int main()
{
    int heap_arr[] = {4,17,3,12,9,6};
```

```
    int n = sizeof(heap_arr)/sizeof(heap_arr[0]);

    cout<<"Input array"<<endl;

    displayArray(heap_arr,n);


    heapSort(heap_arr, n);


    cout << "Sorted array"<<endl;

    displayArray(heap_arr, n);

}
```

Output:

```
Input array

4 17 3 12 9 6

Sorted array

3 4 6 9 12 17
```

Merge Sort

Merge sort algorithm uses the "divide and conquer" strategy wherein we divide the problem into subproblems and solve those subproblems individually.

These subproblems are then combined or merged together to form a unified solution.

Merge sort is performed using the following steps:

- The list to be sorted is divided into two arrays of equal length by dividing the list on the middle element. If the number of elements in the list is either 0 or 1, then the list is considered sorted.

- Each sublist is sorted individually by using merge sort recursively.

- The sorted sublists are then combined or merged together to form a complete sorted list.

General Algorithm

The general pseudo-code for the merge sort technique is given below:

Declare an array Arr of length N

If N=1, Arr is already sorted

If N>1,

Left = 0, right = N-1

Find middle = (left + right)/2

Call merge_sort(Arr,left,middle) => sort first half recursively

Call merge_sort(Arr,middle+1,right) => sort second half recursively

Call merge(Arr, left, middle, right) to merge sorted arrays in above steps.

Exit

As shown in the above pseudo code, in merge sort algorithm we divide the array into half and sort each half using merge sort recursively. Once sub-arrays are sorted individually, the two sub-arrays are merged together to form a complete sorted array.

Pseudo Code for Merge Sort

Following is the pseudo code for merge sort technique. First, we have a procedure merge sort to split the array into halves recursively. Then we have a merge routine that will merge the sorted smaller arrays to get a complete sorted array.

```
procedure mergesort( array,N )

array - list of elements to be sorted

N - number of elements in the list

begin

if ( N == 1 ) return array

var array1 as array = a[0] ... a[N/2]

var array2 as array = a[N/2+1] ... a[N]

array1 = mergesort(array1)

array2 = mergesort(array2)

return merge( array1, array2 )

end procedure

procedure merge(array1, array2 )

    array1 - first array

    array2 - second array

begin

var c as array

while ( a and b have elements )

if ( array1[0] > array2[0] )

        add array2 [0] to the end of c
```

```
        remove array2 [0] from array2
else
        add array1 [0] to the end of c
         remove array1 [0] from array1
end if
end while
while ( a has elements )
add a[0] to the end of c
remove a[0] from a
end while


while ( b has elements )
add b[0] to the end of c
remove b[0] from b
end while


return c
end procedure
```

Let us now illustrate the merge sort technique with an example.

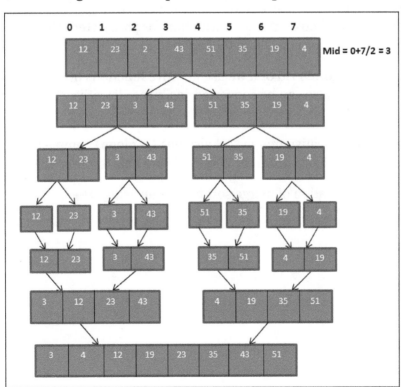

The above illustration can be shown in a tabular form below:

Pass	Unsorted list	divide	Sorted list
1	{12, 23,2,43,51,35,19,4 }	{12,23,2,43}{51,35,19,4}	{}
2	{12,23,2,43}{51,35,19,4}	{12,23}{2,43}{51,35}{19,4}	{}
3	{12,23}{2,43}{51,35}{19,4}	{12,23} {2,43}{35,51}{4,19}	{12,23} {2,43}{35,51}{4,19}
4	{12,23} {2,43}{35,51}{4,19}	{2,12,23,43}{4,19,35,51}	{2,12,23,43}{4,19,35,51}
5	{2,12,23,43}{4,19,35,51}	{2,4,12,19,23,35,43,51}	{2,4,12,19,23,35,43,51}
6	{}	{}	{2,4,12,19,23,35,43,51}

As shown in the above representation, first the array is divided into two sub-arrays of length 4. Each sub-array is further divided into two more sub arrays of length 2. Each sub-array is then further divided into a sub-array of one element each. This entire process is the "Divide" process.

Once we have divided the array into sub-arrays of single element each, we now have to merge these arrays in sorted order.

As shown in the illustration above, we consider each subarray of a single element and first combine the elements to form sub-arrays of two elements in sorted order. Next, the sorted subarrays of length two are sorted and combined to form two sub-arrays of length four each. Then we combine these two sub-arrays to form a complete sorted array.

Iterative Merge Sort

The algorithm or technique of merge sort uses recursion. It is also known as "recursive merge sort"

We know that recursive functions use function call stack to store the intermediate state of calling function. It also stores other bookkeeping information for parameters etc. and poses overhead in terms of storing activation record of calling the function as well as resuming the execution.

All these overheads can be gotten rid of if we use iterative functions instead of recursive ones. The above merge sort algorithm also can be converted easily into iterative steps using loops and decision-making.

Like recursive merge sort, iterative merge sort also has O (nlogn) complexity hence performance wise, they perform at par with one another. We simply are able to lower the overheads.

Given below is an implementation of merge sort technique using C++.

```cpp
#include <iostream>

using namespace std;

void merge(int *,int, int , int );

void merge_sort(int *arr, int low, int high)
{

    int mid;

    if (low < high){
```

```cpp
        //divide the array at mid and sort independently using merge sort
        mid=(low+high)/2;
        merge_sort(arr,low,mid);
        merge_sort(arr,mid+1,high);
        //merge or conquer sorted arrays
        merge(arr,low,high,mid);
    }
}
// Merge sort
void merge(int *arr, int low, int high, int mid)
{
    int i, j, k, c[50];
    i = low;
    k = low;
    j = mid + 1;
    while (i <= mid && j <= high) {
        if (arr[i] < arr[j]) {
            c[k] = arr[i];
            k++;
            i++;
        }
        else {
            c[k] = arr[j];
            k++;
            j++;
        }
    }
    while (i <= mid) {
        c[k] = arr[i];
        k++;
        i++;
    }
```

```
    while (j <= high) {

        c[k] = arr[j];

        k++;

        j++;

    }

    for (i = low; i < k; i++)  {

        arr[i] = c[i];

    }

}

// read input array and call mergesort

int main()

{

    int myarray[30], num;

    cout<<"Enter number of elements to be sorted:";

    cin>>num;

    cout<<"Enter "<<num<<" elements to be sorted:";

    for (int i = 0; i < num; i++) { cin>>myarray[i];

    }

    merge_sort(myarray, 0, num-1);

    cout<<"Sorted array\n";

    for (int i = 0; i < num; i++)

    {

        cout<<myarray[i]<<"\t";

    }

}
```

Output:

```
Enter the number of elements to be sorted:10

Enter 10 elements to be sorted:101 10 2 43 12 54 34 64 89 76

Sorted array

2       10      12      34      43      54      64      76      89      101
```

In this program, we have defined two functions, merge_sort and merge. In the merge_sort function, we divide the array into two equal arrays and call merge function on each of these sub arrays. In merge function, we do the actual sorting on these sub arrays and then merge them into one complete sorted array.

QuickSort

Like Merge Sort, QuickSort is a Divide and Conquer algorithm. It picks an element as pivot and partitions the given array around the picked pivot. There are many different versions of quickSort that pick pivot in different ways:

- Always pick first element as pivot.

- Always pick last element as pivot

- Pick a random element as pivot.

- Pick median as pivot.

The key process in quickSort is partition(). Target of partitions is, given an array and an element x of array as pivot, put x at its correct position in sorted array and put all smaller elements (smaller than x) before x, and put all greater elements (greater than x) after x. All this should be done in linear time.

Pseudo Code for recursive QuickSort function:

```
/* low  --> Starting index,  high  --> Ending index */
quickSort(arr[], low, high)
{
    if (low < high)
    {
        /* pi is partitioning index, arr[pi] is now
           at right place */
        pi = partition(arr, low, high);

        quickSort(arr, low, pi - 1);  // Before pi
        quickSort(arr, pi + 1, high); // After pi
    }
}
```

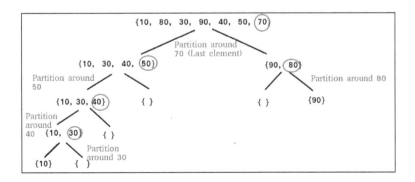

Partition Algorithm

The logic is simple, we start from the leftmost element and keep track of index of smaller (or equal to) elements as i. While traversing, if we find a smaller element, we swap current element with arr[i]. Otherwise we ignore current element.

```
/* low  --> Starting index,  high  --> Ending index */

quickSort(arr[], low, high)

{

    if (low < high)

    {

        /* pi is partitioning index, arr[pi] is now
           at right place */
        pi = partition(arr, low, high);


        quickSort(arr, low, pi - 1);  // Before pi
        quickSort(arr, pi + 1, high); // After pi

    }

}
```

Pseudo Code for Partition()

```
/* This function takes last element as pivot, places
   the pivot element at its correct position in sorted
    array, and places all smaller (smaller than pivot)
   to left of pivot and all greater elements to right
   of pivot */

partition (arr[], low, high)

{

    // pivot (Element to be placed at right position)
    pivot = arr[high];


    i = (low - 1)  // Index of smaller element


    for (j = low; j <= high- 1; j++)

    {
```

```
        // If current element is smaller than the pivot

        if (arr[j] < pivot)

        {

            i++;    // increment index of smaller element

            swap arr[i] and arr[j]

        }

    }

    swap arr[i + 1] and arr[high])

    return (i + 1)

}
```

Partition()

```
arr[] = {10, 80, 30, 90, 40, 50, 70}

Indexes:  0   1   2   3   4   5   6


low = 0, high =  6, pivot = arr[h] = 70

Initialize index of smaller element, i = -1


Traverse elements from j = low to high-1

j = 0 : Since arr[j] <= pivot, do i++ and swap(arr[i], arr[j])

i = 0

arr[] = {10, 80, 30, 90, 40, 50, 70} // No change as i and j

                                     // are same


j = 1 : Since arr[j] > pivot, do nothing

// No change in i and arr[]


j = 2 : Since arr[j] <= pivot, do i++ and swap(arr[i], arr[j])

i = 1

arr[] = {10, 30, 80, 90, 40, 50, 70} // We swap 80 and 30


j = 3 : Since arr[j] > pivot, do nothing

// No change in i and arr[]
```

```
j = 4 : Since arr[j] <= pivot, do i++ and swap(arr[i], arr[j])

i = 2

arr[] = {10, 30, 40, 90, 80, 50, 70} // 80 and 40 Swapped

j = 5 : Since arr[j] <= pivot, do i++ and swap arr[i] with arr[j]

i = 3

arr[] = {10, 30, 40, 50, 80, 90, 70} // 90 and 50 Swapped


We come out of loop because j is now equal to high-1.

Finally we place pivot at correct position by swapping

arr[i+1] and arr[high] (or pivot)

arr[] = {10, 30, 40, 50, 70, 90, 80} // 80 and 70 Swapped


Now 70 is at its correct place. All elements smaller than

70 are before it and all elements greater than 70 are after

it.
```

Implementation

Following are the implementations of QuickSort:

```cpp
/* C++ implementation of QuickSort */
#include <bits/stdc++.h>
using namespace std;


// A utility function to swap two elements
void swap(int* a, int* b)
{
    int t = *a;
    *a = *b;
    *b = t;
}


/* This function takes last element as pivot, places
the pivot element at its correct position in sorted
```

```
array, and places all smaller (smaller than pivot)
to left of pivot and all greater elements to right
of pivot */
int partition (int arr[], int low, int high)
{
    int pivot = arr[high]; // pivot
    int i = (low - 1); // Index of smaller element

    for (int j = low; j <= high - 1; j++)
    {
        // If current element is smaller than the pivot
        if (arr[j] < pivot)
        {
            i++; // increment index of smaller element
            swap(&arr[i], &arr[j]);
        }
    }
    swap(&arr[i + 1], &arr[high]);
    return (i + 1);
}


/* The main function that implements QuickSort
arr[] --> Array to be sorted,
low --> Starting index,
high --> Ending index */
void quickSort(int arr[], int low, int high)
{
    if (low < high)
    {
        /* pi is partitioning index, arr[p] is now
        at right place */
        int pi = partition(arr, low, high);
```

```
        // Separately sort elements before
        // partition and after partition
        quickSort(arr, low, pi - 1);
        quickSort(arr, pi + 1, high);
    }
}


/* Function to print an array */
void printArray(int arr[], int size)
{
    int i;
    for (i = 0; i < size; i++)
        cout << arr[i] << " ";
    cout << endl;
}


// Driver Code
int main()
{
    int arr[] = {10, 7, 8, 9, 1, 5};
    int n = sizeof(arr) / sizeof(arr[0]);
    quickSort(arr, 0, n - 1);
    cout << "Sorted array: \n";
    printArray(arr, n);
    return 0;
}
```

Output:

```
Sorted array:
1 5 7 8 9 10
```

Analysis of QuickSort

Time taken by QuickSort in general can be written as following:

$$T(n) = T(k) + T(n-k-1) + \theta_{(n)}$$

The first two terms are for two recursive calls, the last term is for the partition process. k is the number of elements which are smaller than pivot.

The time taken by QuickSort depends upon the input array and partition strategy. Following are three cases.

Worst Case: The worst case occurs when the partition process always picks greatest or smallest element as pivot. If we consider above partition strategy where last element is always picked as pivot, the worst case would occur when the array is already sorted in increasing or decreasing order. Following is recurrence for worst case.

```
T(n) = T(0) + T(n-1) + Θ(n)
```

which is equivalent to

```
T(n) = T(n-1) + Θ(n)
```

The solution of above recurrence is $\Theta(n^2)$.

Best Case: The best case occurs when the partition process always picks the middle element as pivot. Following is recurrence for best case.

```
T(n) = 2T(n/2) + Θ(n)
```

The solution of above recurrence is $\theta(nLogn)$. It can be solved using case 2 of Master Theorem.

Average Case: To do average case analysis, we need to consider all possible permutation of array and calculate time taken by every permutation which doesn't look easy.

We can get an idea of average case by considering the case when partition puts $O(n/9)$ elements in one set and $O(9n/10)$ elements in other set. Following is recurrence for this case.

```
T(n) = T(n/9) + T(9n/10) + Θ(n)
```

Solution of above recurrence is also $O(nLogn)$.

Although the worst case time complexity of QuickSort is $O(n^2)$ which is more than many other sorting algorithms like Merge Sort and Heap Sort, QuickSort is faster in practice, because its inner loop can be efficiently implemented on most architectures, and in most real-world data. QuickSort can be implemented in different ways by changing the choice of pivot, so that the worst case rarely occurs for a given type of data. However, merge sort is generally considered better when data is huge and stored in external storage.

Radix Sort

The lower bound for Comparison based sorting algorithm (Merge Sort, Heap Sort, Quick-Sort .. etc) is $\Omega(nLogn)$, i.e., they cannot do better than nLogn.

Counting sort is a linear time sorting algorithm that sort in $O(n+k)$ time when elements are in range from 1 to k.

Condition when the Elements are in Range from 1 to n²

We can't use counting sort because counting sort will take $O(n^2)$ which is worse than comparison based sorting algorithms. Can we sort such an array in linear time? Radix Sort is the answer. The idea of Radix Sort is to do digit by digit sort starting from least significant digit to most significant digit. Radix sort uses counting sort as a subroutine to sort.

The Radix Sort Algorithm

Do following for each digit i where i varies from least significant digit to the most significant digit. Sort input array using counting sort (or any stable sort) according to the i'th digit.

Example:

Original, unsorted list:

170, 45, 75, 90, 802, 24, 2, 66

Sorting by least significant digit (1s place) gives: [*Notice that we keep 802 before 2, because 802 occurred before 2 in the original list, and similarly for pairs 170 & 90 and 45 & 75].

170, 90, 802, 2, 24, 45, 75, 66

Sorting by next digit (10s place) gives: [*Notice that 802 again comes before 2 as 802 comes before 2 in the previous list].

802, 2, 24, 45, 66, 170, 75, 90

Sorting by most significant digit (100s place) gives:

2, 24, 45, 66, 75, 90, 170, 802

Running time of Radix Sort

Let there be d digits in input integers. Radix Sort takes $O(d*(n+b))$ time where b is the base for representing numbers, for example, for decimal system, b is 10. What is the value of d? If k is the maximum possible value, then d would be $O(\log_b(k))$. So overall time complexity is $O((n+b) * \log_b(k))$. Which looks more than the time complexity of comparison based sorting algorithms for a large k. Let us first limit k. Let $k <= n^c$ where c is a constant. In that case, the complexity becomes $O(n\log_b(n))$. But it still doesn't beat comparison based sorting algorithms.

What if we make value of b larger? What should be the value of b to make the time complexity linear? If we set b as n, we get the time complexity as $O(n)$. In other words, we can sort an array of integers with range from 1 to n^c if the numbers are represented in base n (or every digit takes $\log_2(n)$ bits).

Implementation of Radix Sort

Following is a simple implementation of Radix Sort. For simplicity, the value of d is assumed to be 10. We recommend you to see Counting Sort for details of `countSort()` function in below code.

```cpp
// C++ implementation of Radix Sort

#include<iostream>

using namespace std;


// A utility function to get maximum value in arr[]

int getMax(int arr[], int n)

{

    int mx = arr[0];

    for (int i = 1; i < n; i++)

        if (arr[i] > mx)

            mx = arr[i];

    return mx;

}



// A function to do counting sort of arr[] according to

// the digit represented by exp.

void countSort(int arr[], int n, int exp)

{

    int output[n]; // output array

    int i, count[10] = {0};


    // Store count of occurrences in count[]

    for (i = 0; i < n; i++)

        count[ (arr[i]/exp)%10 ]++;


    // Change count[i] so that count[i] now contains actual

    //  position of this digit in output[]

    for (i = 1; i < 10; i++)

        count[i] += count[i - 1];


    // Build the output array

    for (i = n - 1; i >= 0; i--)
```

```
    {

        output[count[ (arr[i]/exp)%10 ] - 1] = arr[i];

        count[ (arr[i]/exp)%10 ]--;

    }


    // Copy the output array to arr[], so that arr[] now

    // contains sorted numbers according to current digit

    for (i = 0; i < n; i++)

        arr[i] = output[i];

}



// The main function to that sorts arr[] of size n using

// Radix Sort

void radixsort(int arr[], int n)

{

    // Find the maximum number to know number of digits

    int m = getMax(arr, n);


    // Do counting sort for every digit. Note that instead

    // of passing digit number, exp is passed. exp is 10^i

    // where i is current digit number

    for (int exp = 1; m/exp > 0; exp *= 10)

        countSort(arr, n, exp);

}



// A utility function to print an array

void print(int arr[], int n)

{

    for (int i = 0; i < n; i++)

        cout << arr[i] << " ";

}
```

```
// Driver program to test above functions
int main()
{
    int arr[] = {170, 45, 75, 90, 802, 24, 2, 66};
    int n = sizeof(arr)/sizeof(arr[0]);
    radixsort(arr, n);
    print(arr, n);
    return 0;
}
```

Output:

2 24 45 66 75 90 170 802

References

- Definition-of-algorithm-p2-958013: thoughtco.com, Retrieved 25 June, 2019
- Sorting-and-searching: cprogramming.com, Retrieved 05 January, 2019
- Heap-sort: softwaretestinghelp.com, Retrieved 05 August, 2019
- Merge-sort: softwaretestinghelp.com, Retrieved 15 May, 2019
- Quick-sort: geeksforgeeks.org, Retrieved 16 June, 2019
- Rradix-sort: geeksforgeeks.org, Retrieved 08 July, 2019

6

Data Structures in C++

A data structure is defined as a collection of data which can be easily accessed, managed, combined and modified. C++ uses data structures like stack data structure, queue data structure, heaps, hash tables, two-three trees, binary trees, stacks, linked lists, etc. All these diverse C++ data structures have been carefully analyzed in this chapter.

A data structure is a particular way of organizing data in a computer so that it can be used effectively.

For example, we can store a list of items having the same data-type using the array data structure.

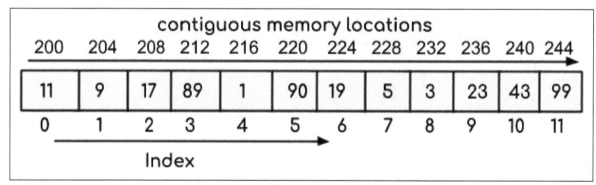

Array Data Structure.

Stack Data Structure

Stack is a fundamental data structure which is used to store elements in a linear fashion. Stack follows LIFO (last in, first out) order or approach in which the operations are performed. This means that the element which was added last to the stack will be the first element to be removed from the stack.

Stack In C++

A stack is similar to real-life stack or a pile of things that we stack one above the other.

Given below is a pictorial representation of Stack.

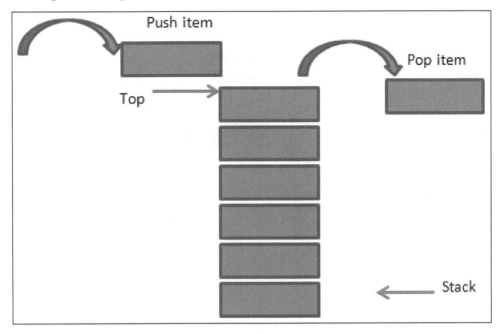

As shown above, there is a pile of plates stacked on top of each other. If we want to add another item to it, then we add it at the top of the stack as shown in the above figure (left-hand side). This operation of adding an item to stack is called "Push".

On the right side, we have shown an opposite operation i.e. we remove an item from the stack. This is also done from the same end i.e. the top of the stack. This operation is called "Pop".

As shown in the above figure, we see that push and pop are carried out from the same end. This makes the stack to follow LIFO order. The position or end from which the items are pushed in or popped out to/from the stack is called the "Top of the stack".

Initially, when there are no items in the stack, the top of the stack is set to -1. When we add an item to the stack, the top of the stack is incremented by 1 indicating that the item is added. As opposed to this, the top of the stack is decremented by 1 when an item is popped out of the stack.

Basic Operations

Following are the basic operations that are supported by the stack:

- Push: Adds or pushes an element into the stack.

- Pop: Removes or pops an element out of the stack.

- Peek: Gets the top element of the stack but doesn't remove it.

- Isfull: Tests if the stack is full.

- Isempty: Tests if the stack is empty.

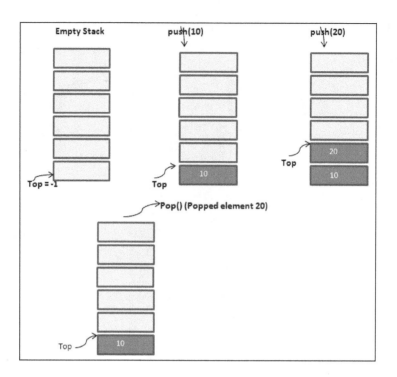

The above illustration shows the sequence of operations that are performed on the stack. Initially, the stack is empty. For an empty stack, the top of the stack is set to -1.

Next, we push the element 10 into the stack. We see that the top of the stack now points to element 10.

Next, we perform another push operation with element 20, as a result of which the top of the stack now points to 20. This state is the third figure.

Now in the last figure, we perform a pop () operation. As a result of the pop operation, the element pointed at the top of the stack is removed from the stack. Hence in the figure, we see that element 20 is removed from the stack. Thus the top of the stack now points to 10.

In this way, we can easily make out the LIFO approach used by stack.

Implementation

Using Arrays

Following is the C++ implementation of stack using arrays:

```
#include<iostream>

using namespace std;



#define MAX 1000 //max size for stack



class Stack
```

```cpp
{
    int top;
    public:
    int myStack[MAX]; //stack array

    Stack() { top = -1; }
    bool push(int x);
    int pop();
    bool isEmpty();
};
    //pushes element on to the stack
    bool Stack::push(int item)
    {
        if (top >= (MAX-1)) {
        cout << "Stack Overflow!!!";
        return false;
    }
else {
    myStack[++top] = item;
    cout<<item<<endl;
    return true;
    }
}


//removes or pops elements out of the stack
int Stack::pop()
{
    if (top < 0) {
        cout << "Stack Underflow!!";
        return 0;
    }
else {
```

```
    int item = myStack[top--];

    return item;

  }

}


//check if stack is empty

bool Stack::isEmpty()

{

   return (top < 0);

}


// main program to demonstrate stack functions

int main()

{

   class Stack stack;

   cout<<"The Stack Push "<<endl;

   stack.push(2);

   stack.push(4);

   stack.push(6);

   cout<<"The Stack Pop : "<<endl;

   while(!stack.isEmpty())

      {

      cout<<stack.pop()<<endl;

      }

   return 0;

}
```

Output

```
The Stack Push

2

4

6
```

```
The Stack Pop:

6

4

2
```

In the output, we can see that the elements are pushed into the stack in one order and are popped out of the stack in the reverse order. This exhibits the LIFO (Last in, First out) approach for the stack.

For the above array implementation of the stack, we can conclude that this is very easy to implement as there are no pointers involved. But at the same time, the size of the stack is static and the stack cannot grow or shrink dynamically.

Using a Linked List

Here, we implement stack operations using a linked list in C++.

```cpp
#include <iostream>
using namespace std;


// class to represent a stack node
class StackNode {
    public:
    int data;
    StackNode* next;
    };


StackNode* newNode(int data) {
    StackNode* stackNode = new StackNode();
    stackNode->data = data;
    stackNode->next = NULL;
    return stackNode;
    }


int isEmpty(StackNode *root) {
    return !root;
    }


void push(StackNode** root, int new_data){
```

```cpp
    StackNode* stackNode = newNode(new_data);

    stackNode->next = *root;

    *root = stackNode;

    cout<<new_data<<endl;

    }


int pop(StackNode** root){

    if (isEmpty(*root))

    return -1;

    StackNode* temp = *root;

    *root = (*root)->next;

    int popped = temp->data;

    free(temp);


    return popped;

}

int peek(StackNode* root)

{

    if (isEmpty(root))

    return -1;

    return root->data;

}


int main()

{

    StackNode* root = NULL;

    cout<<"Stack Push:"<<endl;

    push(&root, 100);

    push(&root, 200);

    push(&root, 300);

    cout<<"\nTop element is "<<peek(root)<<endl;

    cout<<"\nStack Pop:"<<endl;

    while(!isEmpty(root)){

    cout<<pop(&root)<<endl;

}
```

```
cout<<"Top element is "<<peek(root)<<endl;


return 0;

}
```

Output:

```
Stack Push:

100

200

300

Top element is 300

Stack Pop:

300

200

100

Top element is -1
```

Applications of Stack

Let us discuss some of the applications of the stack data structure. The stack data structure is used in a range of applications in software programming mainly because of its simplicity and ease of implementation.

We will briefly describe some of the applications of the stack below:

Infix To Postfix Expressions

Any general Arithmetic expression is of the form `operand1 OP operand 2`.

Based on the position of operator OP, we have the following types of expressions:

- `Infix`: The general form of infix expression is "`operand1 OP operand 2`". This is the basic form of the expression and we use in mathematics all the time.

- `Prefix`: When an operator is placed before the operands, it is a prefix expression. The general form of infix expression is "`OP operand1 operand2`".

- `Postfix`: In postfix expressions, operands are written first followed by the operator. It has the form "operand1 operand2 OP".

Consider the expression "a+b*c". The compiler scans the expression either from left to right or right to left. Taking care of operator precedence and associativity, it will first scan the expression to evaluate the expression b*c. Next, it will again have to scan the expression to add the result of b*c to a.

As the expressions grow more and more complex, this kind of approach of again and again scanning the expression becomes inefficient.

In order to overcome this inefficiency, we convert the expression into postfix or prefix such that they can easily be evaluated using a stack data structure.

Expression Parsing/Evaluation

Using stack, we can also carry out actual expression evaluation. In this, the expression is scanned left to right, and operands are pushed on to the stack.

Whenever an operator is encountered, operands are popped out and the operation is performed. The result of the operation is again pushed into the stack. This way in which the expression is evaluated by using stack and the final result of the expression is usually the current top of the stack.

Tree Traversals

The tree data structure can be traversed to visit each node in many ways and depending on when the root node we have is visited.

- In Order traversal.

- Pre order Traversal.

- Post Order traversal.

To efficiently traverse the tree, we make use of stack data structure in order to push intermediate nodes on the stack so that we maintain the order of traversal.

Sorting Algorithms

Sorting algorithms like quicksort can be made more efficient using the stack data structures.

Towers of Hanoi

This is a classic problem involving n number of discs and three towers and the problem involves moving the discs from one tower to another with the third tower used as intermediate.

This problem can be efficiently tackled using the stack as we push the discs to be moved on to the stack as stack basically acts as a tower used to move the discs.

The Queue Data Structure

The queue is a basic data structure just like a stack. In contrast to stack that uses the LIFO approach, queue uses the FIFO (first in, first out) approach. With this approach, the first item that is added to the queue is the first item to be removed from the queue. Just like Stack, the queue is also a linear data structure.

In a real-world analogy, we can imagine a bus queue where the passengers wait for the bus in a queue or a line. The first passenger in the line enters the bus first as that passenger happens to be the one who had come first.

Queue in C++

In software terms, the queue can be viewed as a set or collection of elements as shown below. The elements are arranged linearly.

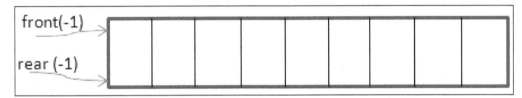

We have two ends i.e. "front" and "rear" of the queue. When the queue is empty, then both the pointers are set to -1.

The "rear" end pointer is the place from where the elements are inserted in the queue. The operation of adding /inserting elements in the queue is called "enqueue".

The "front" end pointer is the place from where the elements are removed from the queue. The operation to remove/delete elements from the queue is called "dequeue".

When the rear pointer value is size-1, then we say that the queue is full. When the front is null, then the queue is empty.

Basic Operations

The queue data structure includes the following operations:

- EnQueue: Adds an item to the queue. Addition of an item to the queue is always done at the rear of the queue.

- DeQueue: Removes an item from the queue. An item is removed or de-queued always from the front of the queue.

- isEmpty: Checks if the queue is empty.

- isFull: Checks if the queue is full.

- peek: Gets an element at the front of the queue without removing it.

Enqueue

In this process, the following steps are performed:

- Check if the queue is full.

- If full, produce overflow error and exit.

- Else, increment 'rear'.

- Add an element to the location pointed by 'rear'.

- Return success.

Dequeue

Dequeue operation consists of the following steps:

- Check if the queue is empty.

- If empty, display an underflow error and exit.

- Else, the access element is pointed out by 'front'.

- Increment the 'front' to point to the next accessible data.

- Return success.

Next, we will see a detailed illustration of insertion and deletion operations in queue.

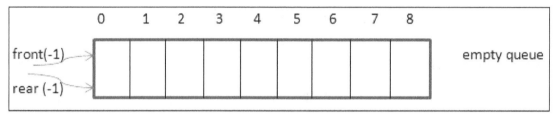

This is an empty queue and thus we have rear and empty set to -1.

Next, we add 1 to the queue and as a result, the rear pointer moves ahead by one location.

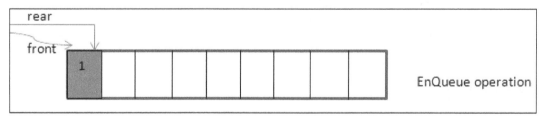

In the next figure, we add element 2 to the queue by moving the rear pointer ahead by another increment.

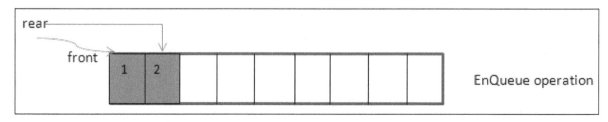

In the following figure, we add element 3 and move the rear pointer by 1.

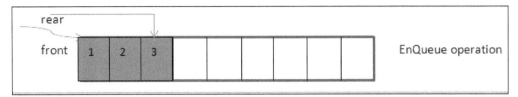

At this point, the rear pointer has value 2 while the front pointer is at the 0th location.

Next, we delete the element pointed by the front pointer. As the front pointer is at 0, the element that is deleted is 1.

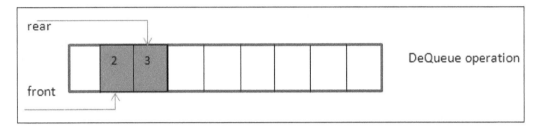

Thus the first element entered in the queue i.e. 1 happens to be the first element removed from the queue. As a result, after the first dequeue, the front pointer now will be moved ahead to the next location which is 1.

Array Implementation For Queue

Let us implement the queue data structure using C++.

```cpp
#include <iostream>

#define MAX_SIZE 5

using namespace std;


class Queue {

private:

int myqueue[MAX_SIZE], front, rear;


public:

Queue() {

front = -1;

rear = -1;

    }


boolisFull() {
```

```
if(front == 0 && rear == MAX_SIZE - 1){

return true;

        }

return false;

    }


boolisEmpty(){

if(front == -1) return true;

else return false;

    }


void enQueue(int value){

if(isFull()){

cout << endl<< "Queue is full!!";

        } else {

if(front == -1) front = 0;

rear++;

myqueue[rear] = value;

cout << value << " ";

        }

    }

int deQueue(){

int value;

if(isEmpty()){

cout << "Queue is empty!!" << endl; return(-1); } else { value = myqueue[front]; if(front
>= rear){        //only one element in queue

front = -1;

rear = -1;

          }

else {

front++;

          }

cout << endl << "Deleted => " << value << " from myqueue";

return(value);

        }

    }
```

```cpp
    /* Function to display elements of Queue */
void displayQueue()
    {
int i;
if(isEmpty()) {
cout << endl << "Queue is Empty!!" << endl;
        }
else {
cout << endl << "Front = " << front;
cout << endl << "Queue elements : ";
for(i=front; i<=rear; i++)
cout << myqueue[i] << "\t";
cout << endl << "Rear = " << rear << endl;
        }
    }
};
int main()
{
    Queue myq;

myq.deQueue();        //deQueue


cout<<"Queue created:"<<endl; myq.enQueue(10); myq.enQueue(20); myq.enQueue(30); myq.
enQueue(40); myq.enQueue(50); //enqueue 60 => queue is full
myq.enQueue(60);


myq.displayQueue();


    //deQueue =>removes 10
myq.deQueue();


    //queue after dequeue
myq.displayQueue();
```

```
return 0;

}
```

Output:

```
Queue is empty!!

Queue created:

10    20    30    40    50

Queue is full!!

Front = 0

Queue elements : 10          20          30          40          50

Rear = 4

Deleted => 10 from myqueue

Front = 1

Queue elements: 20          30          40          50

Rear = 4
```

The above implementation shows the queue represented as an array. We specify the max_size for the array. We also define the enqueue and dequeue operations as well as the isFull and isEmpty operations.

Given below is the Java implementation of the queue data structure:

```java
// A class representing a queue

class Queue

{

int front, rear, size;

int  max_size;

int myqueue[];


public Queue(int max_size) {

this.max_size = max_size;

front = this.size = 0;

rear = max_size - 1;

myqueue = new int[this.max_size];
```

```
    }


    //if size = max_size , queue is full
boolean isFull(Queue queue)
{  return (queue.size == queue.max_size);

    }


    // size = 0, queue is empty
boolean isEmpty(Queue queue)
{  return (queue.size == 0); }


    // enqueue - add an element to the queue
void enqueue( int item)
    {
if (isFull(this))
return;
this.rear = (this.rear + 1)%this.max_size;
this.myqueue[this.rear] = item;
this.size = this.size + 1;
System.out.print(item + " " );
    }
    // dequeue - remove an elment from the queue
int dequeue()
    {
if (isEmpty(this))
return Integer.MIN_VALUE;

int item = this.myqueue[this.front];
this.front = (this.front + 1)%this.max_size;
this.size = this.size - 1;
        return item;
    }
```

```java
    // move to front of the queue
int front()
    {
if (isEmpty(this))
return Integer.MIN_VALUE;

return this.myqueue[this.front];
    }


    // move to the rear of the queue
int rear()
    {
if (isEmpty(this))
return Integer.MIN_VALUE;

return this.myqueue[this.rear];
    }
}


// main class
class Main
{
public static void main(String[] args)
    {
        Queue queue = new Queue(1000);

System.out.println("Queue created as:");
queue.enqueue(10);
queue.enqueue(20);
queue.enqueue(30);
queue.enqueue(40);
```

```
System.out.println("\nElement " + queue.dequeue() +    " dequeued from queue\n");
System.out.println("Front item is " +    queue.front());
System.out.println("Rear item is " +    queue.rear());
    }
}
```

Output:

```
Queue created as:
10    20    30    40
Element 10 dequeued from queue
Front item is 20
Rear item is 40
```

Above implementation is similar to the C++ implementation.

Next, let us implement the queue in C++ using a linked list.

Linked List Implementation for Queue:

```cpp
#include <iostream>
using namespace std;
struct node {
int data;
struct node *next;
};
struct node* front = NULL;
struct node* rear = NULL;
struct node* temp;
void Insert(int val) {
if (rear == NULL) {
rear = new node;
rear->next = NULL;
rear->data = val;
front = rear;
    } else {
```

```
temp=new node;

rear->next = temp;

temp->data = val;

temp->next = NULL;

rear = temp;

    }

}

void Delete() {

temp = front;

if (front == NULL) {

cout<<"Queue is empty!!"<<endl; } else if (temp->next != NULL) {

temp = temp->next;

cout<<"Element deleted from queue is : "<<front->data<<endl;

free(front);

front = temp;

    } else {

cout<<"Element deleted from queue is : "<<front->data<<endl;

free(front);

front = NULL;

rear = NULL;

    }

}

void Display() {

temp = front;

if ((front == NULL) && (rear == NULL)) {

cout<<"Queue is empty"<<endl;

return;

    }

while (temp != NULL) {

cout<<temp->data<<" "; temp = temp->next;

    }

cout<<endl;

}

int main() {
```

```
cout<<"Queue Created:"<<endl;

Insert(10);

Insert(20);

Insert(30);

Insert(40);

Insert(50);

Display();

Delete();

cout<<"Queue after one deletion: "<<endl;

Display();


return 0;

}
```

Output:

```
Queue Created:

10       20       30       40       50

Element deleted from queue is: 10

Queue after one deletion:

20    30    40    50
```

Stack vs. Queue

Stacks and queues are secondary data structures which can be used to store data. They can be programmed using the primary data structures like arrays and linked lists. Having discussed both the data structures in detail, it's time to discuss the main differences between these two data structures.

Stacks	Queues
Uses LIFO (Last in, First out) approach.	Uses FIFO (First in, First out) approach.
Items are added or deleted from only one end called "Top" of the stack.	Items are added from "Rear" end of the queue and are removed from the "front" of the queue.
The basic operations for the stack are "push" and "Pop".	The basic operations for a queue are "enqueue" and "dequeue".
We can do all operations on the stack by maintaining only one pointer to access the top of the stack.	In queues, we need to maintain two pointers, one to access the front of the queue and the second one to access the rear of the queue.
The stack is mostly used to solve recursive problems.	Queues are used to solve problems related to ordered processing.

Applications of Queue

- The queue data structure is used in various CPU and disk scheduling. Here we have multiple tasks requiring CPU or disk at the same time. The CPU or disk time is scheduled for each task using a queue.

- The queue can also be used for print spooling wherein the number of print jobs is placed in a queue.

- Handling of interrupts in real-time systems is done by using a queue data structure. The interrupts are handled in the order they arrive.

- Breadth-first search in which the neighboring nodes of a tree are traversed before moving on to next level uses a queue for implementation.

- Call center phone systems use queues to hold the calls until they are answered by the service representatives.

In general, we can say that the queue data structure is used whenever we require the resources or items to be serviced in the order they arrive i.e. First in, First Out.

Heaps

Heap data structure can be implemented in a range using STL which allows faster input into heap and retrieval of a number always results in the largest number i.e. largest number of the remaining numbers is popped out each time. Other numbers of the heap are arranged depending upon the implementation.

Operations on Heap

- `make_heap()`: This function is used to convert a range in a container to a heap.

- `front()`: This function displays the first element of heap which is the maximum number.

```
// C++ code to demonstrate the working of

// make_heap(), front()

#include<iostream>

#include<algorithm> // for heap operations

using namespace std;

int main()

{
```

```cpp
    // Initializing a vector

    vector<int> v1 = {20, 30, 40, 25, 15};


    // Converting vector into a heap

    // using make_heap()

    make_heap(v1.begin(), v1.end());


    // Displaying the maximum element of heap

    // using front()

    cout << "The maximum element of heap is : ";

    cout << v1.front() << endl;


    return 0;

}
```

Output:

```
The maximum element of heap is : 40
```

3. `push_heap()` : This function is used to insert elements into heap. The size of the heap is increased by 1. New element is placed appropriately in the heap.

4. `pop_heap()` : This function is used to delete the maximum element of the heap. The size of heap is decreased by 1. The heap elements are reorganised accordingly after this operation.

```cpp
// C++ code to demonstrate the working of

// push_heap() and pop_heap()

#include<iostream>

#include<algorithm> // for heap operations

using namespace std;

int main()

{


    // Initializing a vector

    vector<int> v1 = {20, 30, 40, 25, 15};


    // Converting vector into a heap
```

```
    // using make_heap()
    make_heap(v1.begin(), v1.end());


    // Displaying the maximum element of heap
    // using front()
    cout << "The maximum element of heap is : ";
    cout << v1.front() << endl;


    // using push_back() to enter element
    // in vector
    v1.push_back(50);


    // using push_heap() to reorder elements
    push_heap(v1.begin(), v1.end());


    // Displaying the maximum element of heap
    // using front()
    cout << "The maximum element of heap after push is : ";
    cout << v1.front() << endl;


     // using pop_heap() to delete maximum element
    pop_heap(v1.begin(), v1.end());
    v1.pop_back();


    // Displaying the maximum element of heap
    // using front()
    cout << "The maximum element of heap after pop is : ";
    cout << v1.front() << endl;


    return 0;
}
```

Output:

```
The maximum element of heap is : 40
The maximum element of heap after push is : 50
The maximum element of heap after pop is : 40
```

5. `sort_heap()`: This function is used to sort the heap. After this operation, the container is no longer a heap.

```cpp
// C++ code to demonstrate the working of

// sort_heap()

#include<iostream>

#include<algorithm> // for heap operations

using namespace std;

int main()

{


    // Initializing a vector

    vector<int> v1 = {20, 30, 40, 25, 15};


    // Converting vector into a heap

    // using make_heap()

    make_heap(v1.begin(), v1.end());


    // Displaying heap elements

    cout << "The heap elements are : ";

    for (int &x : v1)

        cout << x << " ";

    cout << endl;


    // sorting heap using sort_heap()

    sort_heap(v1.begin(), v1.end());


     // Displaying heap elements

    cout << "The heap elements after sorting are : ";

    for (int &x : v1)

        cout << x << " ";


    return 0;
```

```
The heap elements are : 40 30 20 25 15

The heap elements after sorting are : 15 20 25 30 40
```

6. `is_heap()`: This function is used to check whether the container is heap or not. Generally, in most implementations, the reverse sorted container is considered as heap. Returns true if container is heap else returns false.

7. `is_heap_until()`: This function returns the iterator to the position till the container is the heap. Generally, in most implementations, the reverse sorted container is considered as heap.

```cpp
// C++ code to demonstrate the working of
// is_heap() and is_heap_until()
#include<iostream>
#include<algorithm> // for heap operations
using namespace std;
int main()
{

    // Initializing a vector
    vector<int> v1 = {40, 30, 25, 35, 15};

    // Declaring heap iterator
    vector<int>::iterator it1;

    // Checking if container is heap
    // using is_heap()
    is_heap(v1.begin(), v1.end())?
    cout << "The container is heap ":
    cout << "The container is not heap";
    cout << endl;

    // using is_heap_until() to check position
    // till which container is heap
    auto it = is_heap_until(v1.begin(), v1.end());

    // Displaying heap range elements
```

```
    cout << "The heap elements in container are : ";
    for (it1=v1.begin(); it1!=it; it1++)
        cout << *it1 << " ";


    return 0;
}
```

Output:

```
The container is not heap

The heap elements in container are : 40 30 25
```

Hash Tables

A hash table is a data structure which is used to store key-value pairs. Hash function is used by hash table to compute an index into an array in which an element will be inserted or searched.

This is a C++ program to Implement Hash Tables.

Algorithm

```
Begin
    Initialize the table size T_S to some integer value.
    Create a structure hashTableEntry to declare key k and value v.
    Create a class hashMapTable:
    Create a constructor hashMapTable to create the table.
    Create a hashFunc() function which return key mod T_S.
    Create a function Insert() to insert element at a key.
    Create a function SearchKey() to search element at a key.
    Create a function Remove() to remove element at a key.
    Call a destructor hashMapTable to destroy the objects created by the constructor.
    In main, perform switch operation and enter input as per choice.
    To insert key and values, call insert().
    To search element, call SearchKey().
    To remove element, call Remove().
End.
```

Example Code

```
#include<iostream>
```

```cpp
#include<cstdlib>

#include<string>

#include<cstdio>

using namespace std;

const int T_S = 200;

class HashTableEntry {

    public:

        int k;

        int v;

        HashTableEntry(int k, int v) {

            this->k= k;

            this->v = v;

        }

};

class HashMapTable {

    private:

        HashTableEntry **t;

    public:

        HashMapTable() {

            t = new HashTableEntry * [T_S];

            for (int i = 0; i< T_S; i++) {

                t[i] = NULL;

            }

        }

        int HashFunc(int k) {

            return k % T_S;

        }

        void Insert(int k, int v) {

            int h = HashFunc(k);

            while (t[h] != NULL && t[h]->k != k) {

                h = HashFunc(h + 1);

            }
```

```cpp
        if (t[h] != NULL)

            delete t[h];

        t[h] = new HashTableEntry(k, v);

    }

    int SearchKey(int k) {

        int h = HashFunc(k);

        while (t[h] != NULL && t[h]->k != k) {

            h = HashFunc(h + 1);

        }

        if (t[h] == NULL)

            return -1;

        else

            return t[h]->v;

    }

    void Remove(int k) {

        int h = HashFunc(k);

        while (t[h] != NULL) {

            if (t[h]->k == k)

                break;

            h = HashFunc(h + 1);

        }

        if (t[h] == NULL) {

            cout<<"No Element found at key "<<k<<endl;

            return;

        } else {

            delete t[h];

        }

        cout<<"Element Deleted"<<endl;

    }

    ~HashMapTable() {

        for (int i = 0; i < T_S; i++) {

            if (t[i] != NULL)
```

```
                delete t[i];

                delete[] t;

            }

        }

};

int main() {

    HashMapTable hash;

    int k, v;

    int c;

    while (1) {

        cout<<"1.Insert element into the table"<<endl;

        cout<<"2.Search element from the key"<<endl;

        cout<<"3.Delete element at a key"<<endl;

        cout<<"4.Exit"<<endl;

        cout<<"Enter your choice: ";

        cin>>c;

        switch(c) {

            case 1:

                cout<<"Enter element to be inserted: ";

                cin>>v;

                cout<<"Enter key at which element to be inserted: ";

                cin>>k;

                hash.Insert(k, v);

            break;

            case 2:

                cout<<"Enter key of the element to be searched: ";

                cin>>k;

                if (hash.SearchKey(k) == -1) {

                    cout<<"No element found at key "<<k<<endl;

                    continue;

                } else {

                    cout<<"Element at key "<<k<<" : ";
```

```
                cout<<hash.SearchKey(k)<<endl;
         }
      break;
      case 3:
         cout<<"Enter key of the element to be deleted: ";
         cin>>k;
         hash.Remove(k);
      break;
      case 4:
         exit(1);
      default:
         cout<<"\nEnter correct option\n";
   }
}
return 0;
}
```

Output

```
1.Insert element into the table
2.Search element from the key
3.Delete element at a key
4.Exit
Enter your choice: 1
Enter element to be inserted: 1
Enter key at which element to be inserted: 1
1.Insert element into the table
2.Search element from the key
3.Delete element at a key
4.Exit
Enter your choice: 1
Enter element to be inserted: 2
Enter key at which element to be inserted: 2
1.Insert element into the table
```

2.Search element from the key

3.Delete element at a key

4.Exit

Enter your choice: 1

Enter element to be inserted: 4

Enter key at which element to be inserted: 5

1.Insert element into the table

2.Search element from the key

3.Delete element at a key

4.Exit

Enter your choice: 1

Enter element to be inserted: 7

Enter key at which element to be inserted: 6

1.Insert element into the table

2.Search element from the key

3.Delete element at a key

4.Exit

Enter your choice: 2

Enter key of the element to be searched: 7

No element found at key 7

1.Insert element into the table

2.Search element from the key

3.Delete element at a key

4.Exit

Enter your choice: 2

Enter key of the element to be searched: 6

Element at key 6 : 7

1.Insert element into the table

2.Search element from the key

3.Delete element at a key

4.Exit

Enter your choice: 3

```
Enter key of the element to be deleted: 1

Element Deleted

1.Insert element into the table

2.Search element from the key

3.Delete element at a key

4.Exit

Enter your choice: 4
```

Two-three Trees

The 2-3 tree is also a search tree like the binary search tree, but this tree tries to solve the problem of the unbalanced tree.

Imagine that you have a binary tree to store your data. The worst possible case for the binary tree is that all of the data is entered in order. Then the tree would look like this:

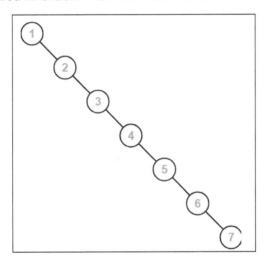

This tree has basically turned into a linked list. This is definitely a problem, for with a tree unbalanced like this, all of the advantages of the binary search tree disappear: searching the tree is slow and cumbersome, and there is much wasted memory because of the empty left child pointers.

The 2-3 tree tries to solve this by using a different structure and slightly different adding and removing procedure to help keep the tree more or less balanced. The biggest drawback with the 2-3 tree is that it requires more storage space than the normal binary search tree.

The 2-3 tree is called such because the maximum possible number of children each node can have is either 2 or 3. This makes the tree a bit more complex, so I will try to explain as much as possible.

One big difference with the 2-3 tree is that each node can have up to two data fields. You can see the three children extending from between the two data fields.

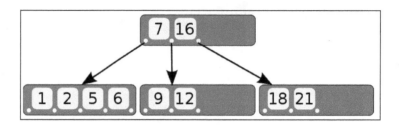

Thus, the tree is set up in the following manner:

- The node must always have a first field, but not necessarily a second field (*data 2*). If both fields are present in a node, the first (or left) field of the node is always less than the second (or right) field of the node.

- Each node can have up to three child nodes, but if there is only one data field in the node, the node cannot have more than two children.

- The child nodes are set so that data in the first sub-tree is less than the first data field, the data of the second sub-tree is greater than the first data field and less than the second data field, and the data of the third sub-tree is greater than the second data field. If there is only one data field in the node, use the first and second children only.

- All leaf nodes appear on the last level.

Now, take a look at the implementation of a 2-3 tree:

```
class twoThreeTree {

  public:

    twoThreeTree(void);        // Constructor

    ~twoThreeTree(void);       // Destructor




    void add(int item);        // Adds an item

    void search(int item);     //

    Searches for an item


  private:

    twoThreeNode *root;        // Pointer to root node



    // Private helper functions go here

};
```

```
class twoThreeNode {

  public:

    int firstData, secondData; // Two data fields


    // The three child nodes

    twoThreeNode *first, *second, *third;


    // This next one is quite useful. It aids

    // moving around the tree. It is a pointer

    // to the parent of the current node.

    twoThreeNode *parent;

};
```

You can see that this tree, unlike the binary search tree or the heap tree, has no remove() function. It *is possible* to program a remove function, but it generally isn't worth the time or the effort.

This tree will be a bit harder to implement than the binary search tree just because of the complexity of the node. Still, the add() function algorithm isn't *that* difficult, and a step-by-step progression through the algorithm helps enormously.

First, to add an item, find the place in the tree for it. This is very much the same as in the binary search tree: just compare and move down the correct link until leaf node is reached.

Once at the leaf node, there are three basic cases for the add() function:

- The leaf node has only one data item: This case is very simple. Just insert the new item after this item or shift the old item forward and insert the new item before the old one, depending on the situation.

- The leaf node is full and the parent node has only one data item: This case is also quite simple. Compare the three values: the two leaf node items and the new item. Choose the middle one and insert it in the parent node where appropriate.

- If the leaf node is the left child, shift the old data in the parent node to the right and insert the middle value in the parent node before the old data. Make sure to shift the pointers *to* the children in the parent node. If the leaf is the right child, just insert the middle value to the right of the old value in the parent node. The two left-over values from the comparison become two leaf nodes, one as the second child, and one as the first or third child depending on the situation.

- Both the leaf node and the parent node are full: This situation is the most complex of all. In the same manner as Case 2, promote the middle value of the leaf node. Then, continue doing the same thing with the parent node, and so on until the situation is resolved or the root node is reached. In this case, the middle value is promoted once again, except a new root node is created from the middle value and the two other values become the left and right subtrees of the new root. At the leaf node at which we began, the new level allows us to split the three initial values into a three node sub-tree of the parent node, and so on.

Doing a few small 2-3 trees by hand helps to understand this algorithm. Remember to check and hold to the rules governing the 2-3 tree! It can get ugly if they are ignored, especially with the last one. Using some recursive helper functions as well as that miraculous parent variable will help ease the pain of programming this tree.

References

- Data-structures: geeksforgeeks.org, Retrieved 28 April, 2019

- Stack-in-cpp: softwaretestinghelp.com, Retrieved 05 August, 2019

- Queue-in-cpp: softwaretestinghelp.com, Retrieved 18 January, 2019

- Heap-using-stl-c: geeksforgeeks.org, Retrieved 19 April, 2019

- Cplusplus-program-to-implement-hash-tables: tutorialspoint.com, Retrieved 05 March, 2019

- Twothree, computersciencetheory: cprogramming.com, Retrieved 26 January, 2019

7

C++ Dialects

A programming language dialect is a small extension of the language that does not changes its nature, but makes it compatible with other programming platforms. This chapter delves into dialects such as Charm++, Embedded C++, R++, Sieve C++ Parallel Programming System, μC++, etc. to provide in-depth understanding of C++ dialects.

Charm++

Charm++ is a machine independent parallel programming system. Programs written using this system will run unchanged on MIMD machines with or without a shared memory. It provides high-level mechanisms and strategies to facilitate the task of developing even highly complex parallel applications.

Charm++ programs are written in C++ with a few library calls and an interface description language for publishing Charm++ objects. Charm++ supports multiple inheritance, late bindings, and polymorphism.

Platforms: The system currently runs on IBM's Blue Gene/Q and OpenPOWER systems, Cray XE6, XK7, and XC40 systems, Infiniband and Omni-Path clusters, clusters of UNIX workstations and even single-processor UNIX, Mac, and Windows machines. It also contains support for running on accelerators such as Xeon Phis and GPGPUs.

The design of the system is based on the following tenets:

- Efficient Portability: Portability is an essential catalyst for the development of reusable parallel software. Charm++ programs run unchanged on MIMD machines with or without a shared memory. The programming model induces better data locality, allowing it to support machine independence without losing efficiency.

- Latency Tolerance: Latency of communication - the idea that remote data will take longer to access - is a significant issue common across most MIMD platforms. Message-driven execution, supported in Charm++, is a very useful mechanism for tolerating or hiding this latency. In message driven execution (which is distinct from just message-passing), a processor is allocated to a process only when a message for the process is received. This means when a process blocks, waiting for a message, another process may execute on the processor. It also means that a single process may block for any number of distinct messages, and will be awakened when any of these messages arrive. Thus, it forms an effective way of scheduling a processor in the presence of potentially large latencies.

- Dynamic Load Balancing: Dynamic creation and migration of work is necessary in many applications. Charm++ supports this by providing dynamic (as well as static) load balancing strategies.

- Reuse and Modularity: It should be possible to develop parallel software by reusing existing parallel software. Charm++ supports this with a well-developed ``module" construct and associated mechanisms. These mechanisms allow for compositionality of modules without sacrificing the latency-tolerance. With them, two modules, each spread over hundreds of processors, may exchange data in a distributed fashion.

The Programming Model

Programs consist of potentially medium-grained processes (called chares), a special type of replicated process, and collections of chares. These processes interact with each other via messages. There may be thousands of medium-grained processes on each processor, or just a few, depending on the application. The "replicated processes" can also be used for implementing novel information sharing abstractions, distributed data structures, and intermodule interfaces. The system can be considered a concurrent object-oriented system with a clear separation between sequential and parallel objects. As shown in this figure, the objects are mapped by the runtime system to appropriate processors to balance the load.

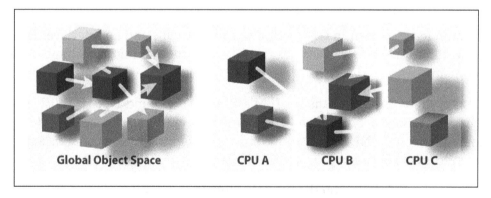

Reusable Libraries: The modularity-related features make the system very attractive for building library modules that are highly reusable because they can be used in a variety of data-distributions. We have just begun the process of building such libraries, and have a small collection of library modules. However, we expect such libraries, contributed by us and other users, to be one of the most significant aspects of the system.

Regular and Irregular Computations: For regular computations, the system is useful because it provides portability, static load balancing, and latency tolerance via message driven execution, and facilitates construction and flexible reuse of libraries. The system is unique for the extensive support it provides for highly irregular computations. This includes management of many medium-grained processes, support for prioritization, dynamic load balancing strategies, handling of dynamic data-structures such as lists and graphs, etc.

Embedded C++

Embedded C++ (EC++) is a dialect of the C++ programming language for embedded systems. It was defined by an industry group led by major Japanese central processing unit (CPU) manufacturers, including NEC, Hitachi, Fujitsu, and Toshiba, to address the shortcomings of C++ for embedded applications. The goal of the effort is to preserve the most useful object-oriented features of the C++ language yet minimize code size while maximizing execution efficiency and making compiler construction simpler. The official website states the goal as "to provide embedded systems programmers with a subset of C++ that is easy for the average C programmer to understand and use".

Differences from C++

Embedded C++ excludes some features of C++.

Feature	ISO/ANSI C C++	Embedded C++
Exception handling	✓	✗
Multiple inheritance	✓	✗
mutable, a storage class specifier	✓	✗
Namespaces	✓	✗
Templates	✓	✗
Run-time type information (typeid)	✓	✗
Style casts (static_cast, dynamic_cast, reinterpret_cast and const_cast)	✓	✗
Virtual base classes	✓	✗

Some compilers, such as those from Green Hills and IAR Systems, allow certain features of ISO/ANSI C++ to be enabled in Embedded C++. IAR Systems calls this "Extended Embedded C++".

Compilation

An EC++ program can be compiled with any C++ compiler. But, a compiler specific to EC++ may have an easier time doing optimization.

Compilers specific to EC++ are provided by companies such as:

- IAR Systems.

- Freescale Semiconductor.

- Tasking Software, part of Altium Limited.

- Green Hills Software.

Criticism

The language has had a poor reception with many expert C++ programmers. In particular, Bjarne Stroustrup says, "To the best of my knowledge EC++ is dead, and if it isn't it ought to be." In fact, the official English EC++ website has not been updated since 2002. Nevertheless, a restricted subset of C++ (based on Embedded C++) has been adopted by Apple, Inc. as the exclusive programming language to create all I/O Kit device drivers for Apple's Mac OS X and iOS operating systems of the popular MacBook, iPhone, and iPad products. Apple engineers felt the exceptions, multiple inheritance, templates, and runtime type information features of standard C++ were either insufficient or not efficient enough for use in a high-performance, multithreaded kernel.

R++

R++ is a rule-based programming language based on C++. The United States patent describes R++ as follows:

> The R++ extension permits rules to be defined as members of C++ classes. The programming system of the invention takes the classes with rules defined using R++ and generates C++ code from them in which the machinery required for the rules is implemented completely as C++ data members and functions of the classes involved in the rules.

R++ was developed by Bell Labs in the 1990s, but due to the Bell System divestiture that split the legal rights to the work developed at the Laboratories between AT&T and Lucent, did not see immediate commercial development while the two companies disputed ownership.

Sieve C++ Parallel Programming System

The Sieve C++ Parallel Programming System is a C++ compiler and parallel runtime designed and released by Codeplay that aims to simplify the parallelization of code so that it may run efficiently on multi-processor or multi-core systems. It is an alternative to other well-known parallelisation methods such as OpenMP, the RapidMind Development Platform and Threading Building Blocks (TBB).

Sieve is a C++ compiler that will take a section of serial code, which is annotated with sieve markers, and parallelize it automatically. The programmer wraps code they wish to parallelise inside a lexical scope, which is tagged as 'sieve'. Inside this scope, referred to commonly as a 'sieve block', certain rules apply:

- All side-effects within the sieve block are delayed until the end of the scope.

- Side-effects are defined to be any modifications to data declared outside the sieve block scope.

- Only functions annotated with sieve or immediate can be called.

Delaying side-effects removes many small dependencies which would usually impede automatic parallelization. Reads and writes can be safely reordered by the compiler as to allow better use of various data movement mechanisms, such as Direct Memory Access(DMA). In addition, alias analysis and dataflow analysis can be simplified. The compiler can then split up code within the sieve block much easier, to exploit parallelism.

Memory Configuration

This separation of scopes also means the Sieve System can be used in non-uniform memory architectures. Multi-core CPUs such as the Cell microprocessor used in the PlayStation 3 are of this type, in which the fast cores have local memories that must be utilized to exploit performance inherent in the system. It is also able to work on shared memory systems, like x86, meaning it can run on various architectures. Sieve blocks can also be nested for systems with a hierarchy of different memories and processing elements.

Parallelization and Scalability

The sieve compiler can split code within a sieve block into chunks either implicitly or explicitly though a 'splithere' statement. For instance, the following example shows parallelizing a loop:

```
sieve
{
    for (iterator i(0); i<length; ++i)
    {
        R[i] = A[i] * B[i]
        splithere;
    }
}
```

The compiler will implicitly add a splitpoint above the for loop construct body, as an entry point. Similarly one will be added after as an exit point.

In the Sieve System, only local variables to the sieve block scope may have dependencies. However, these dependencies must not cross splitpoints; they will generate compiler warnings. In order to parallelize this loop, a special 'Iterator' class may be used in place of a standard integer looping counter. It is safe for parallelization, and the programmer is free to create new Iterator classes at will. In addition to these Iterator classes, the programmer is free to implement classes called 'Accumulators' which are used to carry out reduction operations.

The way the Iterator classes are implemented opens up various means for scalability. The Sieve Parallel Runtime employs dynamic speculative execution when executing on a target platform. This can yield very good speedups, however running on a single core machine can incur overheads.

Determinism

Determinism is an unusual feature of the Sieve System. If executing a parallel Sieve program on a multi core machine yields a bug, the bug will not disappear when run on a single core to aid debugging. This has the advantage of eliminating race conditions, one of the most common bugs in concurrent programming. The removal of the need to consider concurrency control structures within a sieve block can speed up development time and results in safer code.

Supported Systems

The system is designed for hierarchical based systems with homogeneous or heterogeneous CPU cores which have local memories, connected via DMA engines or similar memory transfer models.

Sieve has been shown successfully operating on multi-core x86 systems, the Ageia PhysX Physics Processing Unit, and the IBM Cell microprocessor. ANSI C is generated if a compiler code generator is not available for a certain target platform. This allows for autoparallelization using existing C compilation toolkits.

If you want to make a processor that is capable of processing lots of data (like a video processor for a mobile phone, or a physics processor for a games console) but also uses a small amount of electrical power (so you don't need loud fans or large batteries) then you would make a processor with lots of separate processing units in it. The processing units would do separate parts of the work concurrently. Such a processor is called a multi-core processor.

Multi-core processors provide high levels of processing power for low levels of electrical power consumption. However, existing methods of programming for such devices are time consuming, difficult and unreliable.

Small errors in timing can lead to unpredictable results which means manufacturers of devices with multi-core processors in them tend to be extremely cautious about software testing and reliability. The time taken to write reliable software for multi-core processors leads to high cost and a long time-to-market.

The Ideal Solution

What developers ideally want to be able to do is take a single-core C++ program, pass it through an auto-parallelizing compiler and automatically get out a multi-core program. The resulting multi-core program would be as portable, reliable and easy to debug as the original single-core program. The advantage of this ideal is that the compiler can split up the program among as many cores as are suitable for the project. It would therefore be possible to try out different combinations of cores and clock speeds to get the best performance/power consumption/cost ratios.

Why the Ideal Solution is Impossible

Single-core C++ software contains large numbers of dependencies. Dependencies are situations where one part of the software must be executed after another part of the software. Therefore, the 2 sections cannot be executed at the same time. It might be possible for the programmer to remove those dependencies, either because they are false dependencies or because the algorithm used has dependencies in it (so the programmer would use a different algorithm if they were writing the program for a multi-core processor).

It is therefore impossible for the compiler to automatically change the order of execution of the program to make several parts of the program to be executed at the same time on different processors. Programmer intervention is required. The Codeplay Sieve C++ solution is aimed at reducing to a minimum the extent of such programmer intervention.

The Codeplay Sieve C++ Solution

The programmer marks a section of their program with the "sieve" marker. The resulting section of the program is called a "sieve block". Inside sieve blocks, it is simple and safe for the compiler to perform automatic parallelization.

Inside sieve blocks, side effects are delayed. This means that program code inside sieve blocks can be automatically split into 3 parts: reading data from memory, pure computation and writing data back to memory. Because of this split, the program computation can be parallelized and the memory operations can be separated out parallelized and performed by a DMA system.

The Sieve Concept

The sieve concept is very simple, but has a significant impact on the ability of programmers to write software for parallel systems.

- A sieve is defined as a block of code contained within a sieve {} marker and any functions that are marked with sieve.

- Inside a sieve, all side-effects are delayed until the end of the sieve.

- Side effects are defined as modifications of data that are declared outside the sieve.

These 3 rules have a huge impact on the ability of a compiler to auto-parallelize.

The sieve concept is called "sieve" because it sieves out the side effects from your software and then lets you apply them later.

Here is a trivial example:

```
void simple_loop (float *a,
                  float *b,
                  float f,
                  int n) {
    for (int i=0; i<n; i++)
        { a [i] = b [i] - f;
    }
}
```

This simple C++ loop cannot be safely automatically parallelized by a compiler. There are too many unexplained dependencies in the function, because the 2 pointers 'a' and 'b' could be pointing to memory spaces that overlap.

If we use the sieve concept to parallelize the loop within this function, it looks like this:

```
void simple_loop (float *a, float

    *b, float f, int n) {

    sieve {

        for (int i=0; i<n; i++) {

        a [i] = b [i] - f;

            }

        }    // the assignments to the 'a' array are delayed until here

    }
```

A Sieve C++ compiler can safely automatically parallelize the loop above because of the well-defined meaning of the 'sieve' construct. The assignments to 'a' are being delayed until the end of the loop, so it is safe to transform this loop so that the new array 'a' is calculated in parallel on separate processors and the result stored back to the array 'a' at the end of the sieve block.

Auto-parallelization of Sieve Blocks

C++ programs contain large numbers of dependencies. Dependencies are situations where one section of the program must be executed after other sections of the program. Parallelization requires changing the order of execution. Delaying the side effects removes a huge number of dependencies, which allows the compiler to safely alter the order of execution without breaking the reliable execution of the program. This means that the compiler can automatically split up the program and distribute it amongst multiple processors to be executed at the same time (i.e. re-ordering).

Inside a sieve block, dependencies can only exist on named local variables. Global variables or pointers to external data can never have dependencies inside a sieve block. This means that any dependencies that do still exist inside a sieve block can be identified by the compiler and output in a simple message that the programmer can easily understand. The compiler will print a message saying that there is a dependency on variable 'x' at line n and that the programmer might want to find a way to remove the dependency to increase parallelism. Removing the last few dependencies is essential to achieving parallel execution of the program. So by providing clear, understandable information to the programmer about where the compiler cannot auto-parallelize, the programmer is able to modify the program to be in a form that the compiler can auto-parallelize.

Multiple Memory Spaces with Sieve Blocks

Separating data outside the sieve from data inside the sieve also allows multiple memory spaces to be used. Multiple memory spaces can improve performance of multi-core software by having a different memory space for each processor. Having just one memory space would create a serious memory bottleneck which would stop the multiple processors operating at full speed. By having a separate memory space for each processor, each processor can load and store data from its local memory very quickly. By also providing slower, shared memory spaces, processors can work on shared data. Special Direct Memory Access units (DMA) can be created to quickly transfer data between the different memory spaces. DMA has the advantage over random memory access that it can stream data quickly from large, cheap DRAM.

The data inside a sieve block can be stored on a processor's local memory. The data in main memory that is being read in and written out can be stored in a queue that could be stored in a processor's local memory, main memory or a combination of the two. The actual reading and storing can be performed by a DMA unit.

Using the System in Practice

The process a programmer would use to develop software using the sieve system is:

- Take an existing non-parallel piece of C++ software.

- Identify a section of the software that is suitable for parallelization.

- Mark the section with the sieve marker.

- Mark any functions called by the section with sieve function specifiers.

- Compile the code and fix any errors reported due to mis-matched sieve levels.

- Run and test on a single-core processor.

- Make any adaptations required to keep the program working using sieve semantics.

- Run the compiler in a special mode that advises the user of situations where dependencies are blocking parallelism.

- Use the split/merge system to fix any dependencies reported.

- Compile, run and test on a single-core processor.

- Once working on a single core processor, compile, run, test and performance analyse on a multi-core processor.

- Go back to step 2 if there are any more sections suitable for parallelization.

Extending the Sieve Concept to Parallel Algorithms using Split/Merge

In situations where an algorithm has to change to achieve parallelism, programmers need a way to specify this. A simple example is going through an array of numbers and adding up the numbers to produce a total. On a single-core processor, the programmer would write this:

```
int sum (int *array, int size) {

   int total = 0;

   int index;

   for(index=0; index<size; index++) {

   total += array [index];
```

```
    }

    return total;

}
```

This function cannot be auto-parallelized using just a sieve block, because each iteration of the loop is dependent on the previous iteration. The "total" variable would have to be placed inside the sieve block so that writing to it would not be counted as a "side-effect" and delayed until the end.

The sieve system allows the programmer to create special library classes that can be applied to a local variable to solve this problem:

```
int sum (int *array, int size) {

    int result;

    sieve {

        IntSum total (0) splits result;

        IntIterator index;

        for(index=0;index<size;index++) {

            total += array [index];

        }

    }

    return result;

}
```

The "IntSum" class allows parallel accumulators. Within the class definition are methods that allow the sum operation to be split across multiple processors. The "total" variable is split into several "total" variables, each going to a different processor. At the end of the sieve block, all the "total" variables are supplied to a merge function defined inside the "IntSum" class that adds together all the totals and stores the result in the "result" variable. Because the split/merge algorithm defined here only allows accumulate operations to be performed on "total", the class only defines the "+=" and "-=" operators. It is not legal to read the value of "total" inside the loop. This is the simplest example of an accumulator class. Classes to accumulate trees, lists and other complex data structures can also be defined by the programmer.

The "IntIterator" class allows the "index" variable to be split up and sent to different processors. If the parallel system run-time decides to schedule 10 iterations of the loop on one processor and 10 iterations on another processor, then the value "0" will be assigned to "index" for the first processor and the value "10" for the 2nd . Also, the 1st processor will stop working once the iterator reaches 10. This is the simplest example of a splittable iterator. More complex iterators for lists and trees can also be defined by the programmer.

Both iterators and accumulators would normally be defined by the programmer as templates in header files, so the algorithms could be applied to different data types.

Situations for which the Sieve System is Likely to be useful

Software development for parallel processors. Suitable parallel processors include:

- Multi-core special-purpose processors.

- Special-purpose coprocessors.

- Dual-core or quad-core PC processors.

- Multiple processor server systems.

- Distributed computing environments in which a single application is to be distributed across multiple computers across a network (e.g. a "grid").

- Situations where a processor can be customized to the application. It will be possible to write a single Sieve C++ program and try it out on different combinations of processors, memory sizes and clock speeds to compare power vs performance.

The sieve system is capable of providing portable, scalable software development of complex software on parallel processors.

Sieve Functions

The programmer might want to produce functions that can be called from within sieve blocks. It is not safe to call normal C++ functions immediately inside a sieve block, because the side-effects would have unpredictable effects. For this reason, normal C++ function calls are delayed until the end of a sieve block. This allows functions like "printf" to be called inside sieve blocks and the arguments to the function will be calculated in parallel, but the output will be printed out (in order) at the end.

To call a function immediately inside a sieve block, it must be a sieve function. A sieve function is declared like this:

```
int function (int parameter) sieve;
```

Sieve functions have all their side-effects delayed, like sieve blocks. Because of this, sieve functions can safely be called in parallel. This means that if each iteration of a loop inside a sieve block calls a function, the iterations can be executed in parallel. Even if the sieve function is supplied as a library function without any source code, the compiler can safely parallelize calls to it.

Sieve functions can modify main memory. However, these modifications will be delayed until after the sieve block that called the function.

Immediate Pointers

Sometimes, it is necessary to create complex data structures inside sieve blocks, or to pass variables inside sieve blocks to functions as reference parameters. For this reason, the system needs to have "immediate pointers". Immediate pointers point to data inside the sieve block. Writing to data pointed to by immediate pointers has immediate effect. Therefore, immediate pointers introduce complex dependencies. So the programmer should use them with care. However, they do allow complex structures to be produced inside sieve blocks and stored in fast, local memory.

Immediate pointers are defined as: "`int *0 p;`"

Implementing the Sieve System

The sieve system consists of an extension to a C++ compiler, a multi-core linker and a runtime to schedule the processes.

The extended Sieve C++ compiler compiles the program outside sieve blocks normally. Code inside sieve blocks is separated and compiled according to the sieve rules. Side-effects are extracted and converted into delayed side-effects.

To auto-parallelize, the compiler first determines the dependencies in the sieve block. Dependency analysis is well covered in compiler literature. The difference with sieve blocks, however, is that delayed side-effects can be calculated in any order as long as they end up being applied in the correct order. So, there cannot be any read-after write dependencies to data defined outside the sieve block. This greatly simplifies dependency analysis. In effect, dependency analysis only needs to perform on variables inside sieve blocks and data pointed to be immediate pointers.

The compiler then proceeds to find points in the sieve block where there are no dependencies. If it finds such a point, it is called a "split point".

Often, it will not be possible to find split points without making use of the split/merge operations. Variables defined with split/merge classes (either iterators or accumulators) can have their dependencies removed by calling the merge operation before the split point and the split operation after the split point. Therefore, the compiler can produce more split points by inserting calls to the split and merge operations on the variables to which they apply.

If no split points can be found, then auto parallelization is not safe.

The compiler then takes the sieve block and splits it up into "fragments" of code that start and end at split points (or the start or end of the sieve block). These fragments can be executed in parallel. Fragments have one entry and one or more exit points.

The maximum level of parallelism possible may not be the most efficient implementation, because introducing parallelism involves a fixed cost of calling split/merge operations, sending data and code to a processor, and collecting the results afterwards. So, the compiler will normally take the fragments and re-join them into larger fragments of a size that is known to be optimal for the given architecture.

The sieve system run-time will be invoked on entry to a sieve block. It will be provided with the fragments that were output by the compiler. It will then send those fragments off to the relevant processors. If there are split iterators inside the fragments, then the run-time must choose how many iterations to supply to each processor, giving a start and end iteration count for each.

Because fragments may have more than one exit point, they must return to the run-time which exit point they reached. The run-time can then determine which fragment to execute next.

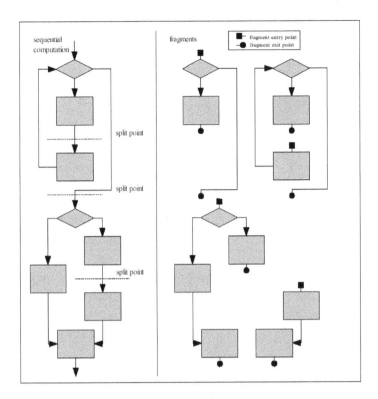

If the run-time executes a fragment with more than one exit point, it cannot know in advance which exit point the fragment will reach. Therefore, it will have to make a choice: either executes the fragments that correspond to each exit point, or wait until the fragment has finished and then execute which ever fragment corresponds to the exit point it did reach. If the run-time chooses the 1st option, it is executing "speculatively". When executing speculatively, it must store the side-effects produced by the speculatively executed fragments in separate queues. When the original fragment returns an exit point, the run-time will finish executing the fragment corresponding to the relevant exit point and apply the side effects returned. The other fragments will be killed and their side-effects queues destroyed.

This speculative execution is inefficient, but increases parallelism dramatically, so improving performance.

Implementing the Sieve Run-time in Hardware

In a typical hardware implementation, there will be a main CPU which has direct access to a main shared memory. All C++ code outside sieve blocks will execute on this processor and use the main shared memory. Code inside sieve blocks will be parallelized onto the custom processors, use the local memory for variables inside the sieve blocks, and use main memory for all heap data and variables declared outside the sieve blocks. A single sieve block can be parallelized onto multiple custom processors with multiple local memories. All memory reads from the custom processors to the main shared memory will happen immediately, either using a load instruction or using a DMA access. All memory writes to the main shared memory occur through a run-time library or DMA unit that can queue up the memory writes and apply them on exit from the sieve block.

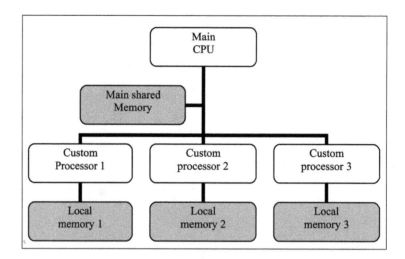

The sieve system operates best if the custom processors can issue memory load instructions from main memory that cannot cause any exceptions or other side-effects. This makes it safe to speculatively issue load instructions, which improves parallelism. Because the main memory is expected to have a high latency, the ability to speculatively issue load instructions early, reduces the impact of the load latency.

If a processor designer wanted to implement the sieve system efficiently in hardware, they could implement the queuing system as a hardware FIFO. Any time a sieve block writes to main memory, the value and address are added to the FIFO. On exit from the sieve block, a DMA unit applies all the memory stores that have been queued in the FIFO to the main shared memory.

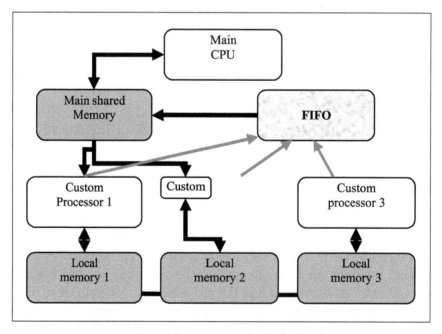

It is not necessary to implement hardware to maintain memory and cache consistency. Because the main memory cannot change while inside a sieve block, the system does not require hardware for maintaining consistency.

Because the sieve C++ compiler outputs small code fragments, it may be possible to implement the code fragments in hardware, as VHDL custom processors, for example. In the simplest case, the custom processors would need hardware to load data from main memory, process the data, and output back to the FIFO.

Impact of the Sieve System on Performance

The sieve system has a benefit and a cost associated with it. The benefit is parallelism. The cost is the overheads of managing the sieve system. The benefits must outweigh the costs for the system to be useful. So the sieve system is suited to high levels of parallelism, or to architectures that map well to the sieve system.

On entry to a sieve block, parallel code sections have to be distributed to processors. Within sieve blocks, stores to memory outside the sieve block must be queued. On sieve block exit, the queued side-effects must be applied before processing on the main CPU can continue. If split/merge classes are used, then the split/merge operations must be called every time a sieve block is parallelized to multiple processors.

One way to reduce the cost of queuing is not to queue. By changing the meaning of sieve blocks to mean that memory writes occur at any time within the sieve block (i.e. out of order) then the cost is removed. However, this removes the determinism of the system and hence makes the system harder to test.

Memory architectures map well to the sieve system. Queued memory stores work well with typical DRAM architectures, and speculative loads hide DRAM load latency. It may even be possible to implement a paged-memory system that allows the processors to continue execution even while queued writes are being applied.

Debugging Sieve C++ Programs

It is possible to create a debugger for Sieve C++ programs. The debugger will be very similar to existing C++ debuggers. It will execute the program in-order, in a single thread, so it will not be necessary for programmers to keep switching between threads to find bugs. The debugger will not interfere with the results of the program. The only change will be that the debugger will show 1 or 2 values for delayed variables – the value that the variable had at the start of the sieve block and (optionally) the value it will have at the end of the sieve block (i.e. the value that it has been assigned within the sieve block).

Advantages of the Sieve System Over OpenMP

OpenMP is an existing system for parallelizing C++ programs. The sieve system is similar, but has some strong advantages:

- OpenMP requires the programmer to provide detailed, correct information about the C++ program supplied. The OpenMP parallelizer needs this information to be correct otherwise the parallelize will produce a program with undefined behaviour. This can cause unreliability.

- The OpenMP parallelizer is not able to check that the information supplied by the programmer is correct, whereas the Sieve C++ parallelizer can check dependency information and provide clear errors and advice about how to make the program more parallel.

- It is possible to debug Sieve C++ programs in a single-threaded environment, but duplicate and fix bugs that exist in multi-threaded execution.

- The Sieve C++ system can handle multiple non-uniform memory spaces. The sieve blocks separate out data into memory spaces. Variables inside sieve blocks go in memory spaces close to the processors, while variables and heap data go in the largest, shared memory space. It is even possible to handle multiple, hierarchical memory spaces.

- The Sieve C++ system can operate with DMA as well as load/store memory architectures.

- The Sieve C++ system can easily use speculative execution, which increases the range of programs that can be parallelized.

μC++

μC++, also called uC++, is a programming language, an extension of C++ designed for concurrent programming. Among other features, it adds coroutines, tasks, and monitors, and extends existing language constructs to integrate with them. Its compiler, named *u++*, operates as a source-to-source translator targeting C++.

μC++ is part of the μSystem project, at the University of Waterloo, Ontario, Canada, a large-scale project led by professor Peter Buhr with the goal to create a "highly-concurrent shared-memory programming system".

It is used in the CS 343 course at the University of Waterloo.

Every μC++ program should include the *uC++.h* header file before any other header, although this is not necessary for more recent versions. uC++ is now open source, available on GitHub.

Keywords

The following keywords are implemented in uC++ to provide extended functionality on class implementations, exception handling capabilities, and scheduling:

- _Accept: Enables external scheduling within monitors. _Accept allows a caller permission to obtain mutual exclusion over a method within the monitor.

- _At: Raises a non-local exception at the argument.

- _CatchResume: Catches an exception but follows the rules of resumption of a caller.

- _Monitor: An extension of a C++ class that permits a class to also operate as a monitor.

- _Cormonitor: An extension of a C++ class that permits use of a class as both a monitor and a coroutine (using suspension and resumption as well as mutual exclusion).

- _Coroutine: An extension of a C++ class that permits coroutine based functionality.

- _Enable: Enables non-local exception handling within a task.

- _Disable: Disables non-local exception handling within a task (default).

- _Event.

- _Mutex: Enables mutual exclusion on a class member.

- _Nomutex: Disables mutual exclusion on a class member.

- _Select: Allows blocking on wait for access to a future (Future_ISM<T>, Future_ESM<T>).

- _Resume.

- _Task: An extension of a C++ class with its own stack and thread control; mutually exclusive by default.

- _Throw: Allows non local exception throwing.

- _When: An argument condition to an accept statement similar to a condition.

Permissions

Index

Printed in the USA
CPSIA information can be obtained
at www.ICGtesting.com
JSHW051418221024
72173JS00006B/1374